DEFEAT
AND DISARMAMENT

DEFEAT
AND
DISARMAMENT

Allied Diplomacy
and the Politics
of Military Affairs
in Austria, 1918–1922

JOE C. DIXON

Newark: University of Delaware Press
London and Toronto: Associated University Presses

Associated University Presses
440 Forsgate Drive
Cranbury, NJ 08512

Associated University Presses
25 Sicilian Avenue
London WC1A 2QH, England

Associated University Presses
2133 Royal Windsor Drive
Unit 1
Mississauga, Ontario
Canada L5J 1K5

The paper used in this publication meets the
requirements of the American National Standard for
Permanence of Paper for Printed Library Materials Z39.48-1984.

Library of Congress Cataloging in Publication Data

Dixon, Joe C.
    Defeat and disarmament.

    Bibliography: p.
    Includes index.
    1. Austria—Military policy.   2. Austria—Politics
and government—1918–1938.   3. Austria—History, Military.
I. Title.
UA670.D59   1986   355'.0335'436   82-49193
ISBN 0-87413-221-5 (alk. paper)

Printed in the United States of America

Contents

Preface

Military affairs in the First Austrian Republic have not attracted a great number of scholars. The literature on the first Federal Army in the twenty years between 1918 and 1938 pales compared with that on the monarchy's army during the four years of its last war.[1] Notable among the handful who have looked at the Austrian army in the interwar period is Ludwig Jedlicka, late head of the *Institut für Zeitgeschichte* at the University of Vienna. His book, published in 1955, on the army in the "shadows of party politics" remains the only full-length study on the Federal Army between the wars.[2] It accords only light treatment, however, to the early years of the Republic.

In sheer numbers as well as political potential, the legal Austrian army was dwarfed by paramilitary "defense" organizations on the Left and on the Right. The protofascist groups in particular have attracted historians. C. Earl Edmondson's monograph on the Austrian *Heimwehr* includes an excellent bibliography that details the best of the large body of literature dealing with right-wing movements in Austria.[3] Socialist formations have received less attention, perhaps because the Left was crushed by the Right in 1934. Most published accounts of the socialist *Schutzbund* are penned by apologists, notably Otto Bauer, Julius Deutsch, and Julius Braunthal. There exists no significant study dealing specifically with disarming paramilitary groups in the early years of the republic.[4]

The vast body of literature on the Paris Peace Conference of 1919 includes very little on Austrian military issues. Most studies on Austria at the peace conference focus upon political, territorial, and economic issues.[5] The invaluable publication by Almond and Lutz on the Treaty of Saint Germain addresses only nonmilitary terms of the settlement.[6] Harold W. V. Temperley

7

addresses some military issues, but his useful comments are nonetheless brief.[7] The official report of the Austrian delegation at the Peace Conference is the best published source on military issues, but the army question is clearly secondary to political and economic issues.[8]

Given, therefore, the relative paucity of published works on Austrian military affairs in the First Republic, and the lack of any publications on Austrian disarmament as an international issue, a study of the subject seems appropriate. A wealth of primary sources is available today in several countries that was not available to Jedlicka in 1955. The passage of time, as always, has provided the possibility of a different perspective. Finally, the insight gained by subsuming Austrian military affairs under the general theme of disarmament promises to clarify, if only a little, the tragic saga of Europe's attempt and failure to make peace with itself after the self-destruction of the Great War of 1914.

The years 1918–22 constitute a distinct period in Austrian interwar history. With the inauguration of government under the strong hand of Chancellor Ignaz Seipel in May 1922, a period of economic recovery—thanks to a loan from the League of Nations—and political domination by conservatives replaced conditions of political uncertainty and economic chaos. This monograph focuses on 1918–22, when many of the questions about Austria's future political, economic, social, and military character were yet unanswered.

This study would not have been possible without the support and guidance of many people. Messieurs Peter Sugar, Gunther Rothenberg, Béla Király, Alfred Hurley, and David Spires provided invaluable assistance in selecting and defining this project. Special thanks go to Professor Robert Kann, who provided welcome advice and counsel to me in Vienna.

My brief but productive visit to the U.S. National Archives indebted me to Tim Nenninger in the Navy and Old Army Branch. An equally brief stopover at the new British Public Record Office in Kew netted rich rewards, thanks to patient and expert help from R. R. Mellor and F. F. Lambert.

In Austria, my list grows longer. Frank Forgione of the American Embassy and Anton Porhansl of the Fulbright Commission aided my orientation to Vienna. Captain Bruce Boevers (U.S. Army) and his wife, Mary, not only provided friendship but gave me quick insights into the maze of the University of Vienna. No one there provided more help and encouragement than Dr. Karl Haas of the *Institut für Zeitgeschichte*.

All who work in the *Kriegsarchiv* must sing the praises of Herr Leopold Moser, director of the library, self-taught in many languages and friend of all who enter his domain. His greatest service, perhaps, was introducing me to Manfried Rauchensteiner of the *Heeresgeschichtliches Museum (Wissenschaftliches Institut)*. Dr. Rauchensteiner showed great patience with an American ignorant of the most elementary facts, and led me deftly to the most useful sources in Vienna. His generosity included not only his professional expertise but the hospitality of his home. These gentlemen were complemented by the helpful staff members of the *Verwaltungsarchiv* and the *Haus-, Hof-, und Staatsarchiv*. Special thanks go to Dr. Horst Brettner of the *Neues Politisches Archiv*.

The efficiency of the staff at the Hoover Institution in Stanford, California, is matched only by the richness of the documents collected there. And last, but hardly least, I salute the friendly people in the Air Force Academy Library, especially Mrs. Betsy Coleman, interlibrary loan librarian.

My greatest debt is to those who offered advice and comment on this work as it progressed. Lieutenant Colonel Carl Reddel provided valuable comments on early chapters. Major Harry Borowski read early drafts and always found time in a busy schedule to discuss at length the mysteries of Austrian history. Foreign Service Officer Edward Brynn permitted me to push friendship to its limits; his patient, profound, and elegant comments from a remote posting in West Africa saved me from innumerable errors. Thanks also go to my former professor at the University of Minnesota, William E. Wright of the Center for Austrian Studies, who guided the dissertation upon which this study is based. Finally, acknowledgement is due John M. Thompson, Distinguished Visiting Professor at the Air Force Academy, for helping me polish the final manuscript.

Without the cooperation, encouragement, and help of my wife, Barbara, this project would not have been possible. It is as much hers as it is mine. The errors and shortcomings of this study, of course, are mine alone.

Introduction

The theme of this study is disarmament in Central Europe after the Great War of 1914–18, with a focus on Austria. Military affairs in Austria usually take a secondary position in historical literature to the more perilous problem of German military affairs, or more pressing Austrian postwar problems, such as the food shortage, financial instability, union with Germany *(Anschluss),* and boundary disputes. This study attempts to rescue from obscurity the story of Austrian military affairs, a story only partially told heretofore, at least in English.

The Great War of 1914–18 constitutes a major turning point in world history, a major watershed in European history. Western Europe, profoundly shaken, clung desperately to major institutions and old traditions; Central and Eastern Europe were transformed practically beyond recognition. A new order emerged where once ruled Romanov, Hohenzollern, and Habsburg. Authoritarian rule in the Russian Empire, the German Empire, and the Dual Monarchy of Austria-Hungary gave way in 1917 and 1918 to forms of government that rested, in theory, upon rule by the people. The watchword, self-determination, meant not only a voice in self-government, but the right to form a state composed of one's own ethnic brethren. Newly independent nation-states, created in the image of the victors in the war, emerged from the ruins of three broken empires.

The Baltic countries (Estonia, Latvia, Lithuania) and Finland appeared as independent states on the new map of 1918. Poland enjoyed a dramatic resurrection, claiming with a vengeance territories formerly held by all three dynasties, and rekindling the ancient enmity of both Germany and Russia. On the ruins of the Habsburg monarchy new polities arose: Czechoslovakia, darling of the west; Rumania, enlarged beyond all expectations; and the new Serb-Croat-Slovene state, christened Yugoslavia. The

11

losers were Austria and Hungary, the former a tiny collection of alpine provinces bearing the name but little resemblance to the empire from which it sprang, and the latter reduced to a third of its former size and harboring sentiments of revenge against all its neighbors, none of whom failed to profit at Magyar expense. A republican Germany was created, seething with discontent. And to the east, the Soviet inferno broiled, ever threatening to send a Bolshevik tide crashing and rolling across a prostrate Europe.

The war aims of the belligerents had changed and become more precise during the course of the Great War. By war's end, the Western powers had all adopted in various degrees the Wilsonian vision of fighting unlimited war for universal and permanent peace. The Great War became the "war to end all wars" and the "war for democracy." The peacemakers who gathered in Paris in January 1919 saw only too clearly the similarities between the Paris Peace Conference and the great Congress of Vienna, which had shaped the peace settlement of 1815 after the Napoleonic Wars in the nineteenth century. The twentieth-century diplomats and politicians took great pains, however, to convince themselves, and those who would listen, that the settlement of 1919 was different, and that it was based upon lofty principles of self-determination, democracy, and hope for permanent peace through the League of Nations.

In retrospect, one of the greatest differences proved to be the most unfortunate. In 1815, the defeated power, France, had been admitted as a partner to the deliberations of the Great Powers. In 1919, the defeated powers, notably Germany and Austria, were excluded from the victors' councils. The Paris peace settlement, ostensibly based on high principles of justice, has come to be the classic case of a vindictive settlement that brings not peace, but war. The Versailles Treaty imposed upon Germany was sharply criticized by German and non-German alike. The Nazi rise to power would certainly have been more circuitous and much less likely had the terms of the treaty not engendered strong currents first of hopelessness and then of resentment in the German people.

Great Britain, France, Italy, and the United States dominated the peace conference. Plenary sessions including lesser powers were merely public forums wherein decisions by the Big Four were announced. The Supreme Council, later the Council of Four or simply the "Council," included David Lloyd George of Britain, Georges Clemenceau of France, Vittorio Emanuele Orlando of Italy, and Woodrow Wilson of the United States. Supporting these four leaders were a myriad of committees and study groups that submitted reports and recommendations to the Council of Four.

The Versailles settlement with Germany loomed as the victors' main concern. Germany's lesser partners in the war, Austria-Hungary, Bulgaria, and Turkey, were peripheral to the main problem. However, the fact that Austria-Hungary—an empire of more than fifty million—no longer existed did not prevent the victorious powers from imposing a victor's peace upon the newly formed republic of "German-Austria" and the rump state of Hungary. The tiny, emaciated state of Austria contained only six and a half million people, most of whom were German-speaking, and who were to share with the Hungarians blame and retribution for the Habsburg role in the war.

The monarchy on the Danube with its capital at Vienna had been a polyglot creation of the Habsburg dynasty, including Serbs, Croats, Slovenes, Czechs, Slovaks, German-Austrians, Poles, Italians, Magyars, Rumanians, and Ruthenes. In 1918 the monarchy split into its component parts. The German-speaking people who composed the new state of Austria inherited the enmity and hatred that other nationalities had directed earlier against the Habsburg dynasty and its Danube capital. Coal for Austrian industry and food for Vienna came from outlying provinces in Bohemia, Moravia, and Silesia, and from the rich lands of Hungary. With the monarchy's collapse, Vienna found its lifelines cut. Rampant inflation of Austrian currency compounded the economic distress.

Distrust and even hatred of Vienna were not confined to former "subject" nationalities. The conservative, religious population of rural western Austria had reserved its loyalty for the Habsburg dynasty, not the industrial cities of eastern Austria, and especially not the godless socialist stronghold of Vienna. When the dynasty disappeared, the western provinces sought to detach themselves from Vienna and join their Swiss, Bavarian, and even Italian neighbors. No more enthusiastic about an Austrian state than the peasants, socialist and middle-class politicians in Vienna declared their intentions to unite with their German brothers to the north. The victorious Western powers, however, denied Austrians the right of self-determination. After all, how could the winners in the war allow the loser, Germany, to emerge from the war larger and more powerful than she had been in 1914? Independence was imposed upon Austria. The birth of Austria saw the creation of a "state that nobody wanted."[1]

The politics of the unwanted republic were inherited from the monarchy. The Austrian Parliament, recalled by Kaiser Karl in May 1917, contained a confusing array of political parties and national groupings from all parts of the Austrian half of the Dual Monarchy. Deputies from the German-speaking districts, which would form the new Austrian republic in 1918, generally sorted themselves into three major political groups: Social Democrats, Christian Socials, and German Nationalists.

The Social Democratic Party had been founded by Viktor Adler in 1889 as a Marxist socialist party. It was characteristically committed to taking power through the ballot box, not by violent revolution. Although it contained various factions and its members frequently held sharply opposing views, the party maintained a remarkable sense of unity. It clearly dissociated itself from the tiny Communist Party in Austria that emerged in 1918. The Social Democrats' main power-base was in Vienna.

The second major party was the Christian Social Party, brought to prominence in Vienna by Karl Lueger and others in the 1890s. In its early years the party represented the interests of the lower bourgeoisie. By 1918, however, its character had changed somewhat as a result of numerous electoral alliances with more conservative and clerical groups, until the Christian Social Party emerged as a conservative Catholic party and one of the main supports of the crown. In the new republic the party's chief adherents were in the countryside and its main powerbase was in western Austria, although it still enjoyed considerable support in urban areas. The party found it hard to keep the peasant and urban wings united.[2]

The third major political grouping was more a tradition than a political party, and carried a variety of labels. Three of the most common were German Nationalists, Pan-Germans, and All-Germans.[3] The party in 1918 was an amalgam of groups that had grown out of the Linz Program of 1882, a litany of demands by German liberals for restoration and maintenance of the predominance of the German element in the multinational Habsburg monarchy. On the fringe of the party in the late nineteenth century, Georg von Schönerer preached an extreme creed of Pan-Germanism that combined elements of anti-clericalism, racial anti-Semitism, and a revolutionary variety of anti-Habsburg German nationalism. The Pan-Germans wanted to rid themselves of the Slavic component in their midst by attaching German areas of the Austrian Empire to Bismarck's German Empire. Schönerer's brand of German chauvinism met with only limited success, however, at least until the Hitler era. The mainstream of German Nationalists in the monarchy before 1918 sought only to maintain a special place for German language and culture within the Habsburg realm and usually offered a milder form of anti-Semitism than that characteristic of Schönerer's followers. Before the war, the party's position on union with Germany was not always clear; after 1918, the party generally championed *Anschluss*. The German Nationalists' main base of support was the urban middle and upper classes, although they gained considerable support in the rural areas after the monarchy's collapse. The party's program favored liberalism and progress, freedom from state control, and strong doses of anticlericalism and anti-Semitism.

The German Nationalists and the Christian Socials were considered the two "bourgeois" parties in Austria, even though both drew much support from the peasant class.[4] The main sources of disagreement between the two parties were the Nationalists' anticlericalism and disdain for the Habsburgs. After 1918 the Habsburg issue faded, but *Anschluss* became more controversial. The German Nationalists resented any roadblocks that prevented union with Germany or reunion with Germans in Czechoslovakia. The Christian Socials gave only lukewarm support to *Anschluss* in the early months of the republic, and opposed it in later years.

From the beginning of its existence, the Austrian republic was a ward of the Great Powers. Food and economic assistance were funneled from Italy, France, Great Britain, America, and even Germany. The Western powers could and did enforce their will in Austria by threatening to cut off food or economic credits. Financial assistance, in particular, was usually dependent on Austrian promises not to seek union with Germany.

But Austria was not without a weapon of her own. The Bolshevik Revolution in Russia had badly frightened many Western leaders; the brief rule of Béla Kun in Soviet Hungary during the spring and early summer of 1919 confirmed the worst suspicions in the West. More than once, the Austrian leaders of all parties raised the spectre of Bolshevik rule in Austria should Austrian demands not be met. More often than not, Austria gained concessions from the worried West.

Distrusted by its neighbors, forced to exist against its will, the state of Austria led an unhappy existence between the wars. The political parties sought not only to win elections over their opponents, but to crush completely their ideological foes. Harsh economic conditions spawned radical political solutions to difficult problems. Paramilitary groups threatened class warfare. Democracy fared no better in Austria between the wars than anywhere else in Central Europe.

Democracy can function smoothly only where there is agreement on fundamentals, where at least a substantial majority is willing to abide by the rules of the political game. . . . These conditions simply did not exist in the Successor States, or to a sufficient degree in the last years of prewar Austria. Every party and ethnic group was loyal only to itself and in the Successor States regarded rivals as mortal enemies who had to be denied access to power.[5]

Neither the noble hope for universal peace, nor even the less ambitious goal of stability in Central Europe, would be realized after 1918. Civil war threatened to break out from the earliest days of the Austrian republic, and finally did so in 1934, marking the end of representative democracy in the country. Four years later, Hitler answered the *Anschluss* question by force of arms. A year after that, the people of Austria were engulfed in the life-and-death struggle of Hitler's Thousand Year Reich. The hopes and dreams of 1918 were completely shattered by 1939.

Abbreviations and Terms

The following list of abbreviations and terms includes those used in note citations. For a more complete reference, see the Bibliography.

BAFR: British Attaché's Fortnightly Report. See F. O. below.

BMfA: Bundesministerium für Äusseres (Federal Ministry for Foreign Affairs). See *StAfA* below.

BMfHW: Bundesministerium für Heerwesen (Federal Ministry for Military Affairs, later called *Bundesministerium für Heereswesen*). See *StAfHW* below.

BMfI: Bundesministerium für Inneres (Federal Ministry for the Interior).

BMfU: Bundesministerium für Unterricht (Federal Ministry for Education).

C.A.: Conference of Ambassadors, Minutes of Meetings.

C.F.: Council of Four, Minutes of Meetings.

DBFP: Documents on British Foreign Policy, 1919–1939. First Series. (London, 1947ff.)

d.-österr.: Deutsch-Österreich (German-Austria).

F.O.: Foreign Office documents, from British Public Record Office.

FRUS: Papers Relating to the Foreign Relations of the United States, 1918. (Washington, D.C., 1930.)

FRUS-PPC: Papers Relating to the Foreign Relations of the United States: The Paris Peace Conference 1919. (Washington, D.C., 1942–1947.)

H.D.: Council of the Heads of Delegations, Minutes of Meetings.

ICC: Inter-allied Control Commission(s).

KabProt: Kabinettsprotokolle (Records of Cabinet Meetings).

Liq. Org.: Liquidation Organ.

M-xx, roll x: Microcopy number and microfilm roll number from the National Archives of the United States, Record Group 256.

NPA Karton: Box of documents, *Neues Politisches Archiv,* Vienna.

PdöW: "Provisorische deutschösterreichische Wehrmacht, 1918–1920," a collection of documents in the *Kriegsarchiv,* Vienna.

PPC-DB: Daily Bulletins issued by the Military Information Section at the Paris Peace Conference, found at the Hoover Institution.

StAfA: Staatsamt für Äusseres (Ministry of Foreign Affairs).

StAfHW: Staatsamt für Heerwesen (Ministry for Military Affairs).

StenProt, Konst. Nationalversammlung d.-österr.: Official records of the proceedings of the German-Austrian Constituent Assembly.

StenProt, Prov. Nationalversammlung d.-österr.: Official records of the German-Austrian Provisional Assembly.

StRProt: Staatsrat Protokolle (Records of State-Council Meetings).

ZGBh: "Zur Geschichte des Österreichischen Bundesheers," a collection of documents in the *Kriegsarchiv,* Vienna.

DEFEAT
AND DISARMAMENT

1

Collapse of the Old Order

THE fortunes of war in 1914 were not kind to the Habsburg monarchy in the opening round of hostilities. Habsburg losses in Serbia during the first six months of the war were nearly 100,000 men, a shocking and embarrassing defeat at the hands of a small country that Austria-Hungary had intended to punish quickly and easily. The campaign against the Russians was even bloodier. In the face of unexpected Russian strength and staggering losses in men, by mid-September the Habsburg chief of staff, Conrad von Hötzendorf, was forced to abandon Galicia and seek refuge for his armies in the Carpathian Mountains. Better than one in three Austro-Hungarian troops employed during a month's fighting in Galicia had been killed, wounded, or taken prisoner. Even worse, the toll was heavy among trained officers and noncommissioned officers. The old professional army, so long a mainstay of the monarchy, simply "died in 1914."[1]

The Habsburg recovery from the military disasters of 1914 was a remarkable achievement. Having lost the flower of the professional army in the first months of the war, the monarchy managed to refurbish its military forces in 1915 and by the end of 1916 had mobilized five million men, formed twenty new divisions, and reequipped field and heavy artillery.[2] Much has been made of Germany's two-front war in 1914–18; few remember that after Italy joined the fray in 1915 the Habsburg monarchy faced war on three fronts: the eastern front in Galicia and the Carpathians; the Italian front; and the Balkan front, where for a time Austria-Hungary (with German help) secured control over parts of the peninsula "never fully overpowered by ancient Roman legions, by Turkish conquerors, or by the armies of Napoleon I."[3]

The Russian armies were badly mauled and pushed well back into Russian territory in 1915 by combined German and Austrian attacks. But a stubborn rear-guard action frustrated the German and Austrian strategic goal of encircling and crushing the Russian armies. Despite losing Warsaw and central Poland and most of Galicia, the Russian armies remained intact, though severely weakened, at the end of a sometimes brilliant withdrawal. Furthermore, German successes in the north and center of the 600-mile front, which ran from the Baltic Sea to the Rumanian border, were not matched by Austro-Hungarian achievements in the south, where Russian forces under General Brusilov still held parts of eastern Galicia.

The following year brought mixed fortunes to both sides and exhaustion to all. The Brusilov Offensive in 1916 on the Russian southwest front against Austro-Hungarian forces opened in June and enjoyed early success. The Habsburg forces had been thinned by Conrad's grandiose plans for an Italian offensive, and the Germans were preoccupied with the Battle of Verdun in the West. German reinforcements from East Prussia eventually bolstered the Austrian defense, along with Austrian troops withdrawn from the canceled Italian offensive; Brusilov was finally stopped in September. He had achieved impressive tactical gains but had failed to achieve strategic success: the Habsburg Empire was still alive and fighting. Most observers concur that the cost and ultimate failure of the Brusilov Offensive shattered morale in the Russian army and helped push the country closer to the brink of revolution. Nonetheless, the Russian sacrifice forced Conrad to postpone his offensive against Italy, and very well may have saved the French at Verdun.

Meanwhile, the poor showing against Brusilov convinced Franz Josef to give in to German demands for a unified command on the eastern front. Hindenburg was given command of the entire front except for an army group under the nominal command of the Habsburg Archduke Karl. The value of the unified command was demonstrated against the hapless Rumanians, whose ill-timed entry into the war in August 1916 was too late to help Brusilov. Rumania collapsed by December. If nothing else, success against the Rumanians gave the dying Habsburg emperor some comfort in his last days. Franz Joseph's death in November 1916 brought to the throne his grand-nephew Karl, a young man woefully inadequate to handle the overwhelming problems before him.

Internal upheavals within Russia overshadowed fighting on the eastern front in 1917. Brusilov did mount an offensive in June under the Provisional Russian Government, but it was a poor imitation of the offensive of the summer before. By the end of July, Kerensky had to admit that Russian armies in the southwest could advance no further. German attacks in the north hastened the disintegration of Russian armies. The Bolshevik Revolution and subsequent armistice in the east freed Habsburg troops for the Italian front, which by 1917 had turned into a bloody war of attrition, not unlike the western front in France and Belgium.

The Italian campaign, more than any other, inspired the peoples of the Habsburg monarchy. Italian claims to the Trentino enraged the patriotic Tyrolese, and South Slavs fought the Italians enthusiastically in the northern Adriatic. Italy began its offensive in May 1915 the day after declaring war on the Dual Monarchy. A series of Italian offensives toward the Isonzo River were attempted from 1915 to 1917 in hopes of capturing Trieste. Although the Italians made some gains, notably in 1916 when Brusilov was hammering the monarchy from the other side, the eleven separate Battles of the Isonzo accomplished little but destroy Italian morale in a reckless orgy of blood-letting. But Austro-Hungarian losses were heavy, too, and the monarchy could ill afford a long war. Consequently, in the autumn of 1917, after Brusilov's second offensive sputtered out in the east, German and Austro-Hungarian reinforcements were sent to the Italian front. Under German guidance, Habsburg and German armies crushed the demoralized Italian army at the Battle of Caporetto. By November the Italians had been pushed back across the Piave River with more than 300,000 causalties, most of them taken prisoner in the confusion of the rout. The Central Powers lost only 20,000 men killed and wounded.

At the end of 1917 the new Habsburg emperor could survey triumph in the east over Russia and Rumania, great success in the Balkans, and a good showing against Italy. But the cost had been high; the Habsburg war effort was now directed from Berlin, and signs of discontent within the monarchy were growing more ominous. Military rule in domestic affairs played no small part in provoking the rising wave of revolution from within. Military forces, with German help, had emerged victorious on the battlefield. But they lost the war at home.

There were two facets to the military's role within the monarchy. Insensitive suppression of Czechs and South Slavs led to increasing Slavic disaffection from the Habsburg state. The second facet included control of economic life and management of factories in particular. For German-speaking Austrians, the army's management of industrial activities, confiscation of property, and arbitrary punishment of those who were uncooperative, were the most offensive wartime activities.

None of the powers that went to war in 1914 correctly predicted the enormity of economic problems they would encounter. And the government of Franz Josef was not alone in developing the machinery of a war economy. The Habsburg apparatus, however, was probably less successful than the Western powers in enlisting the voluntary sacrifices required by a whole people at war. By the end of 1917, military authorities not only lost the early influence they had enjoyed in civil affairs, but their policies had thoroughly alienated the nationalities and thereby contributed to the very disaster in 1918 they had sought to prevent.

The Habsburg military picture never looked brighter than in January 1918, when Austro-Hungarian forces were everywhere victorious and stood everywhere on enemy soil; by November both the monarchy and its army had disappeared. The changes wrought in the wake of the Danubian monarchy's collapse were certainly revolutionary, but the upheaval was hardly a classic revolution. The existing government was not overthrown violently, as it had been in France in 1789, or in Russia in 1917, or even routed temporarily as it had been from Vienna in 1848. Rather, in October and November 1918, the monarchy simply turned over the reins of power to its successors and invited them to rule as they wished. The only blood spilled in this revolution resulted from squabbles among the successors. One Viennese wag, it is said, distributed a leaflet which announced that on the morrow at eleven o'clock there would be a revolution, and "in case of rain the revolution will take place indoors."[4] The story may be apocryphal, but nonetheless captures the essential flavor of the Austrian Revolution in October.

The genesis of the Austrian Revolution goes back at least to the wave of industrial strikes that began in the Daimler works on

14 January 1918 at Wiener Neustadt south of Vienna, and spread rapidly throughout the industrial areas of Austria, to Budapest, and eventually to Berlin and other major German cities. The spark that lit the flame was a reduction in food rations, which were already meager. Once begun, the strike movement grew to include greater demands. At the instigation of socialist and trade union leaders, the striking workers elected local workers' councils, more or less on the Soviet model. The councils voiced complaints about scant food rations, censorship, long working hours, military courts and discipline, and even the imprisonment of Friedrich Adler, socialist assassin of Prime Minister Stürgkh in 1916. The chief demand, however, perceived as the root cause of the trouble, was for the war to end. A joint declaration by the socialists and trade union leaders included warnings to the government that the workers insisted upon quick conclusion of the peace negotiations with Trotsky at Brest-Litovsk, and a settlement based on the principle of national self-determination. The strike movement lasted only a week before it was suppressed by Habsburg military authorities, but the government did grant some political concessions. Promises included revision of electoral laws and reopening peace talks with the Russians. The newly formed workers' councils continued in a reduced and semiunderground form until they reemerged at the end of the war.[5] Ironically, the Habsburg policy of subduing the population by force played into the hands of radical national leaders, including German-Austrian socialists, by giving them the "breathing space" they needed to consolidate their control of the revolutionary situation that had been brought on by acute food problems and Bolshevik propaganda.[6]

The armies of the Austro-Hungarian monarchy withstood four long, devastating years of war far better than friend or foe had expected. In his last weeks, Franz Josef insisted that peace must come by 1917; he had long been pessimistic about victory. But in early 1918 the Habsburg military machine was still a formidable instrument.

Even for domestic opponents and doubters, the army at this moment [beginning of 1918] still commanded respect. It was unbroken, confident, and had thrust deeply into conquered territory in the Ukraine, the Balkans, and Upper Italy, thereby meriting a position to share in dictating peace on the eastern front.[7]

By spring, however, signs of trouble appeared within the army in spite of the apparently strong position of the Austrians on the Italian front. The March peace treaty with Bolshevik Russia freed Habsburg forces on the eastern front for action elsewhere, but it also set free thousands of prisoners of war who returned home to the monarchy infused with Marxist ideas. Trotsky had used the negotiations at Brest-Litovsk to give a wide dissemination to Bolshevik slogans for peace. The returning prisoners of war had also been a target of Bolshevik propaganda, and caused serious disruption within the Habsburg army once they returned home.

The Bolshevik ideological offensive was not the only one, nor was it ultimately the most dangerous, faced by Habsburg officials. Agitation from the West fed nationalist aspirations that had already grown by leaps and bounds during the war. The Allied propaganda offensive begun in April 1918 was the second onslaught in that year on the morale of the Austro-Hungarian military forces. Eventually, the appeal of popular government and national self-determination proved stronger than the appeal of Lenin's Bolshevism.

Revolts and mutinies in the armed forces in 1918 exhibited varying degrees of national and social aims. The desertion of the Second Brigade of Pilsudski's Polish Legion under General Haller in February 1918 and the exploits of the famous Czech Legion are obvious examples of activity inspired by national aims. Nationalist themes emerged from the leadership of the naval mutiny in the Habsburg Fifth Fleet anchored in the Gulf of Cattaro, although other grievances also played a part. Less clear, however, was the mutiny of the Seventeenth Infantry Battalion in Styria in May. The mostly Slovene unit captured an ammunition dump and spread disorder, proclaiming a program that reflected both social and national aims:

> . . . the war must be ended now, whoever is a Slovene, join us. We are going home; they should give us more to eat and end the war; up with Bolsheviks, long live bread, down with the war.[8]

At least four other disturbances took place in May. The Seventh Jäger at Murau was incensed by insufficient food and by agitation of returned prisoners from Russia. Former prisoners of war also played a part in the revolt of the Ruthene Fifty-Eighth

Battalion at Ljubljana. A largely Serbian unit mutinied at Pécs on 20 May, and a day later Czech troops mutinied at Rumberg, refusing to fight until they received pay for the time they had been held prisoners.[9]

Finally, four years after the war began, the fears of military commanders were being realized. Less and less could commanders count on non-German or non-Magyar soldiers. Nevertheless, Conrad, who had been demoted by the young emperor from chief of staff to a position as commander on the Italian front, planned a great offensive against the Italians designed to bring them to their knees in the summer of 1918. He was not successful; the Habsburg forces were denied a second Caporetto. The June offensive was broken by surprising Italian tenacity, heavy flooding along the Piave River, and war weariness in the Habsburg lines.

The June battles along the Piave marked clearly the end of any hopes that Austria-Hungary could prevail militarily; the only hope for survival was immediate cessation of hostilities. The sad fact is that German and Austrian authorities realized in mid-summer the war could not be won, but fought on until surrender in November.[10]

Suspicion among the general population that the monarchy was doomed turned to firm belief in September when it took the Entente only sixteen days from the opening of a new Balkan offensive to knock Bulgaria completely out of the war. Long pentup hopes, fears, and aspirations broke loose in October, death-month of the ancient monarchy.

In the last year of the monarchy's existence, German-speaking delegates to Parliament were subjected to increasingly hostile speeches and declarations by non-German delegates. By early October 1918, the rising wave of sentiment for national self-determination had become a flood tide. Bowing to the inevitable, and taking the lead in this as in so many other matters, the German-Austrian Social Democrats recognized the rights of other nationalities to self-determination. They also claimed the right of German-speaking Austrians to establish an independent state and determine their own destiny. The following day, 4 October, the German Nationalists enthusiastically announced their agreement with the general principles of the Social Democratic resolution. The Christian Socials were more reluctant to break with their imperial past, but events were soon to push them in that direction.[11]

The Central Powers sent a request on 4 October via the Swedish government to President Wilson for an immediate armistice and negotiations based on the Fourteen Points.[12] Five days later the Christian Socials reluctantly followed the lead of the other German-Austrian parties by acknowledging the right of self-determination for all nations of the Dual Monarchy. Refusing to abandon the Habsburgs, however, the Christian Socials optimistically predicted that the natural outcome of self-determination would be a federation of free national communities.[13]

Wilson deliberately delayed answering the Austro-Hungarian request for an armistice until 19 October.[14] In the meantime, endless schemes for federalization and reform of the Habsburg monarchy were discussed in Vienna. The emperor's Manifesto—a quixotic attempt at revolution from above—was published on 16 October 1918. Alas, it was too late; neither the empire's nationalities nor its enemies in war were impressed by empty promises, delivered by a powerless ruler, to federalize the empire. The October Manifesto simply accelerated centrifugal forces already in motion. Julius Andrassy, Habsburg foreign minister, remarked that "in order that no one else should annihilate us, we determined upon suicide."[15]

Vienna learned of Wilson's reply on 20 October 1918; the answer was more ominous than Austria's worst fears. The fate of the empire was put into the hands of its Czechoslovak and South Slav members.[16] The Czechs, with nominal Slovak support, had already declared their independence, and the Yugoslavs were moving rapidly in the same direction. Despair overtook friends of the monarchy.

The next day, 21 October, 210 German-speaking members of the Imperial Parliament assembled in Vienna and declared themselves to be the Provisional National Assembly of independent "German-Austria."[17] The new German state, to be built upon the principle of self-determination, claimed all former Habsburg territory populated by German-speaking people, especially the Sudeten districts of Bohemia. The Provisional Assembly assumed the right to represent citizens in the new state until a Constituent National Assembly, elected by the people, would adopt a constitution for the nation. No decision was made in October on the future form of government, since the parties were divided over the issue. The Social Democrats expressed their preference for a democratic republic; the Christian Socials and the German Nationalists favored a constitutional monarchy.[18] As a temporary expedient, the assembly selected an executive committee of twenty to represent the new state in dealings with foreign nations and with the old government of the Austrian Empire, which had not yet passed from the scene. Representatives of the Provisional National Assembly soon made contact with the imperial cabinet; the first meeting of the Lammasch Ministry on 28 October was interrupted by the arrival of representatives from the provisional government.[19] On 31 October, Prime Minister Lammasch informed the provisional government that he had been empowered to transmit to it the agenda of the emperor's cabinet on matters concerning German-Austria.[20] For the next several days Vienna was treated to the quite unrevolutionary spectacle of old and new governments working side by side with the highest level of cooperation. Old and new ministers worked in the same office or across the hall from one another as the newcomers assumed their functions. Officials in the imperial bureaucracy continued to function, without interruption, under the new government.

At the second meeting on 30 October the Provisional National Assembly adopted a provisional constitution drawn up by Karl Renner, the Social Democrat destined to be the first Austrian chancellor in 1919 and also the first president in the Second Republic after World War II. Under Renner's plan, the Assembly was the sole legislative body. The executive committee of twenty, to be called a State Council, would have an executive directorate of five: three presidents (one from each party), a director of the chancery, and a notary. Renner was chosen "director" of the chancery, a sort of head of government.[21] The next day the State Council appointed a ministry of thirteen, including a Ministry for Military Affairs, and assumed for itself the supreme military power in the new state, although the new government hoped to dissociate itself from the Habsburg war by refusing any participation in armistice-negotiations.

Activity in the provinces matched the activities of the Provisional Assembly in Vienna. In Linz on 31 October a mass demonstration was followed by the formation of a Soldiers' Council. A provisional government for Upper Austria, based on the political distribution of the election in 1911, was organized on 3 November. A few days earlier, a People's Council in Salzburg, representing all political parties, had agreed to establish a provisional government for the province. Tyrolean separatism was implicit in the very name chosen there: the Tyrolean National

Council. Formed on 26 October by political parties, trade unions, and other organizations, the National Council led to a provisional government for the Tyrol based on 1914 elections. Vorarlberg separated itself from the Tyrol and organized a government with three provincial presidents chosen from the three major parties. In Graz, a "Welfare Committee" was set up on 21 October with the chief task of distributing food. This Welfare Committee led to the formation of a provisional government for Styria that represented the three parties equally. And, finally, the parties in Carinthia formed a provisional executive committee, and a provisional assembly met in Klagenfurt.[22]

Both the old imperial cabinet and the new State Council debated the question of what to do with the emperor during the first days of November. The State Council found itself under increasing pressure to proclaim a republic immediately rather than wait for the Constituent Assembly to decide on the form of the state. There were noisy street demonstrations in Vienna in favor of a republic and growing signs from outlying provinces that sentiment throughout the country favored a republic.[23] On 11 November, after news of the German kaiser's abdication, the State Council decided to submit to the Provisional Assembly a law proclaiming German-Austria a republic. The Council agreed that this was the only hope for maintaining the fragile coalition and preventing anarchy in the streets.[24]

Meanwhile, the imperial cabinet sought ways to complete the process of turning over the administration to the new government and to vote itself out of existence. The Lammasch ministry, installed on 22 October, considered itself to be a liquidation cabinet whose duty it was to disassemble the old government as peacefully as possible. On the evening of 10 November, Renner and Karl Seitz, another Social Democrat in the State Council, urged Lammasch to persuade the emperor to abdicate in order to keep revolutionary fervor under control. On the following day, Emperor Karl issued a manifesto that was deliberately vague and that fell short of a formal abdication, although it soon came to have the same effect.[25]

Since my accession I have been untiring in my efforts to lead my peoples out of the horrors of the war, for whose outbreak I bear no blame. I have not delayed the restoration of constitutional existence and have opened to the peoples the way to their independent state development. Now as ever filled with unalterable love for all my peoples, I will not oppose my person as a hindrance to their free development.

I recognize in advance the decision German-Austria takes with reference to its form of state in the future. The people, through its representatives, has taken over the government. I renounce every participation in the business of state. At the same time I remove my Austrian government from office.

May the people of German-Austria create and consolidate the new organization in harmony and in a conciliatory spirit. The happiness of my peoples was from the beginning the aim of my warmest wishes. Only internal peace can heal the wounds of this war.[26]

The following day, 12 November 1918, the Provisional National Assembly of German-Austria approved the passage of a law drafted by the State Council. The law proclaimed the new state to be a republic, abolished privileges of the Habsburg family, dissolved parliamentary bodies of the monarchy, set elections for a Constituent National Assembly for February 1919, and declared the German Austrian Republic a part of Germany.[27]

The transition from old to new, from empire to republic, proved to be a remarkably smooth one, not marred by the bloodshed of the German Revolution that occurred at the same time. But there had been threats of violence from both sides in Austria. Julius Deutsch spent day and night restraining soldiers of the Vienna garrison who wanted to occupy government buildings and forcibly eject the remaining vestiges of the Habsburg government.[28] On the other side, Habsburg Field Marshal Boroević had assembled loyal troops from the defeated Isonzo army in Klagenfurt and in the first week of November was ready to march on Vienna to save the emperor. Boroević sent two telegrams to the emperor, begging him to authorize action. The emperor did not comply, and Boroević's plans came to nothing.[29] The heroic deeds in 1848 of Windischgrätz, Radetzky, and Jelačić would not be duplicated in 1918.

The relatively tranquil transition in political life provides a surrealistic background to the violent, tragic fate that befell the Habsburg army in Italy. The Habsburg army on the Italian front in October and November 1918 provides one of the most remarkable stories in the annals of war. Thousands died in a desperate attempt to save an empire that had already ceased to exist. However—even though political collapse preceded military defeat—the empire's internal disintegration was hardly the sole reason for defeat.

Battles in June on the Piave had broken the spirit of the Habsburg army. In July the high command estimated that the fifty-seven divisions in Italy actually had a combat effectiveness equal to only thirty-seven divisions.[30] The army's effectiveness deteriorated further throughout the autumn of 1918. Food became so scarce that reserves frequently "deserted" to the front lines, where rations were slightly better.[31] Tattered rags served as uniforms, providing little protection against cold and rain. Disease and starvation took a terrible toll; malnourished men had little defense against malaria in the coastal plain or influenza in the numbing mountain cold.[32] Morale, already low, plummeted in September when Bulgaria collapsed and the Balkan front was transformed into a Hungarian front.

The emperor's Manifesto of 16 October shattered what little spirit the army had left. The emperor's promise to reconstruct the empire along federal lines was widely interpreted to mean that the people of the empire were free to form immediately their own national states. Shortly afterward, Hungarian Prime Minister Tisza made the stunning public announcement, "We have lost the war." On 20 October, the new Károlyi government in Hungary demanded that Hungarians return home from the Italian front. The army was disintegrating rapidly as men of all nationalities streamed home in droves.

On 23 October, Magyar and South Slav troops in Boroević's normally reliable Army Group announced they would fight no longer; they wanted only to go home. The following day, the Entente finally opened its long-awaited offensive against the remnants of the Habsburg army. By that time, twenty-one of the fifty-seven Habsburg divisions in Italy contained units that refused to obey any orders.[33] Incredibly, the Austrian defense was tenacious for two days, and in places the Austro-Hungarian troops even counterattacked. The lull on the fourth day gave weary soldiers a chance to reflect on their condition as mail from home reached the trenches.

> . . . Now their mail packets from home revealed the true state of affairs in the hinterland. Now the trench rumors were confirmed; the independent states of what was once the

monarchy were calling all of their men home. Word of mutiny, revolt, and desertion was passed along from unit to unit.[34]

The renewed Entente offensive, spearheaded by French and British soldiers, met little resistance after the fourth day, as Habsburg units abandoned their equipment and fled the battlefield for their homes.

> Hungarian, Croatian, Czech, and finally even German-Austrian formations demanded to be transported home, refusing to go into action, mutinied, and on occasion fought officers and still-loyal units.[35]

It is very difficult to put a respectable face on the "glorious" Italian victory at Vittorio Veneto. Contemporary British and American observers were unanimous in their scorn for the Italian effort, a sentiment reflected in A. J. P. Taylor's sarcastic description of the offensive:

> . . . Finally, on November 3, the Austro-Hungarian high command, negotiating in the name of an Empire which no longer existed, concluded an armistice of surrender with the Italians. After the armistice had been signed, but before it came into force, the Italians emerged from behind the British and French troops, where they had been hiding, and captured hundreds of thousands of unarmed, unresisting Austro-Hungarian soldiers in the great "victory" of Vittorio Veneto.[36]

The offensive launched against the hapless Austrian forces was, of course, consistent with the original Italian motives for entering the war. Three years of fighting had not earned Italy the undisputed right to acquire territory promised in the Treaty of London.[37] In place of victory, Italy had suffered frustrating stalemate and then crushing defeat at Caporetto. The Italian Command needed a military victory to secure Italy's claim to a prominent place in the peace negotiations; Vittorio Veneto was the best that could be done.

Early in October, in anticipation of the war's end, the Austrian chief of staff, Arz, had ordered the formation of an armistice commission under General Viktor von Weber.[38] The commission languished in Trent through most of the month, awaiting the emperor's decision to initiate talks. Finally on 28 October, Arz and Emperor Karl directed the armistice commission to initiate contact with the Italians and to conclude an immediate armistice. Any concession was to be granted that "did not infringe upon the honor of the army or constitute an outright capitulation."[39] Such instructions may have been realistic earlier; by the end of October anything short of surrender would not satisfy the Entente.

It was not until 31 October that the commission was allowed to cross the Italian lines. The Entente terms were presented at Villa Guisti near Padua: (1) "immediate" suspension of hostilities; (2) complete demobilization, immediate withdrawal of all troops, a postwar Austrian army limited to twenty divisions, and surrender of half of all artillery equipment including all such war matériel in territories evacuated by the Austrians; (3) evacuation of territory occupied since 1914 as well as additional territory including the South Tyrol, with all military and railway equipment including coal within the evacuated areas to be left in place and surrendered to the Allied and Associated Powers; (4) occupation rights for the victors, including free movement throughout Austria-Hungary; (5) complete evacuation of German troops from Austro-Hungarian territory within fifteen days; (6) immediate repatriation without reciprocity of all Allied prisoners of war; (7) surrender without compensation of the entire Austro-Hungarian fleet to the victors; (8) and continuation of the blockade against Austria.[40]

Arz was stunned by the severity of the terms.[41] Upon learning of the terms in Paris, Clemenceau remarked, "There is one thing omitted. You have not demanded the Emperor's breeches."[42]

The emperor had no choice but to accept the terms, yet—typically—spent two days agonizing over the decision. The Hungarians were more decisive; on 1 November, the pacifist Károlyi government ordered all Hungarian troops to put down their arms. The Austro-Hungarian high command was helpless to prevent the Hungarian message from reaching the front, and could do little but warn Hungary that she was responsible for the consequences of her action.[43] Finally, at 11:30 P.M. on 2 November, Karl gave General von Weber approval to sign the terms as presented.

At 2:00 in the morning of 3 November, Arz sent a telegram to all commanders informing them that armistice terms had been accepted and that all hostilities were to cease immediately. Fifteen minutes later, perhaps realizing the full significance of what he had done, he sent a second message canceling the first, but it was too late to correct the damage. Habsburg units ceased all operations as the Italians continued the war.

In the afternoon on 3 November, the delegations met at Villa Guisti to sign the armistice. The Italians calmly told von Weber it would be impossible to inform all Italian units of the cease-fire in less than twenty-four hours. The horrified Austrians had little choice but to sign. The Italians continued operations against surprised and nonresisting Habsburg troops until 4 November. Since soldiers who were behind the front lines when the armistice took effect (4 November) were to be considered prisoners of war, motorized Italian units moved rapidly to secure the deepest possible penetration during the twenty-four-hour "grace" period. Curious Austrian soldiers, little suspecting they would soon be taken prisoner, simply watched the former enemy drive past. The uncontested Italian advance netted some 350,000 prisoners.[44]

As disgusting as the Italian performance may appear, the blame must fall upon the Habsburg high command. Some even argue that the "mistake" was deliberate, that Austrian authorities preferred masses of hungry, armed, and undisciplined soldiers to be taken prisoner rather than roam the Austrian countryside on a wild rampage.[45] In any case, whether by design or simply through stupidity, the army came to an ignominious end.

The Italians did not, of course, capture the whole army. Even those units behind the lines that retained discipline and arms had little trouble threatening their captors and simply marching away.

> Everywhere the story was the same. Those units that had lost cohesion or had given up their weapons were rounded up and herded into prisoner of war camps. Those units that had maintained their discipline and marched back fully armed were sometimes stopped, but if they refused to surrender they were allowed to continue on towards home.[46]

Thousands upon thousands of soldiers streamed home by any available means. The trains, which miraculously continued to function in the absence of central governmental authority, were filled to overflowing. The haunting spectacle of men riding on the tops of railroad cars and losing their lives as trains passed through low tunnels, or under low bridges, finds its way into almost every account of the army's pell-mell "Drang nach Hause."[47] Soldiers discarded equipment and frequently threw away all arms when they reached the supposed safety of Austria. Individually or in units, they hurried across a land in which there was no authority to guarantee law and order.

The Habsburg army was never formally demobilized.[48] It simply melted away. Neither the old nor the new government in Austria had the means or the will to contain the army's spontaneous disintegration. In the wake of the army's sudden disappearance, the civil authorities had little means of ensuring the population's safety. The search for security would present the new government in Vienna with one of its most pressing problems in the months ahead.

2

Creation of the *Volkswehr*

THE Austrian story in the winter of 1918–19 provides a striking contrast to the German experience. The structure of the German army, especially its high command, survived the war intact to form an uneasy partnership with the new socialist German government. The body of the Habsburg army vanished practically overnight before the eyes of a broken Austro-Hungarian high command. The problem was not how to control the Habsburg army, but how to replace it.

The basic decisions on armed forces in Austria, however, were not in Austrian hands. Domestic discussions and plans for the future were futile exercises until the Paris Peace Conference made and publicized its decisions. That was not to happen until the summer of 1919.

In late October 1918 it was not yet obvious that the Habsburg army would dissipate in a few weeks. The general expectation was that in one way or another the new regime would assume control over the existing army. Speaking to a German-Austrian delegation on 25 October, the monarchy's war minister recognized the right of the successor states, including German-Austria, to build their own armies from the men and matériel of the fallen imperial forces. He cautioned, however, against an overhasty dissolution.[1]

The Provisional National Assembly was prompted to act on 30 October when the Habsburg high command confessed that the War Ministry could no longer protect German-Austrian territory and could not guarantee preservation of peace and order within. As a result, the Assembly created the Ministry for Military Affairs *(Staatsamt für Heerwesen)*, which took over the functions

37

of the old imperial offices of war, navy, and defense. The Assembly declared that all members of the Imperial Army from German-speaking districts were to come under the jurisdiction of the new administration of German-Austria. Control of military forces was to reside only in the government; no private "national guards" were to be organized. Where local groups had already formed protective associations, steps should be taken to bring these "civil guards" usder the authority of the new provisional government.[2]

The government clearly needed to gain control over existing military organizations or see to it that they were disbanded and disarmed. During the Provisional Assembly's second meeting on 30 October, a crowd of officers and enlisted men gathered out front. Part of the crowd proceeded to the Imperial War Ministry, and there selected a delegation headed by an artillery lieutenant. The newly formed delegation returned to the Assembly and recommended the creation of a German-Austrian army. The Assembly politely suggested that the rag-tag group would be consulted in future deliberations concerning an army for the new state. Undaunted, spokesmen for the soldiers promised to establish contact with various other military groups the following day. After excited deliberations, a group of soldiers, including a strong party advocating a Republican Red Guard, decided to form a soldiers' council of three officers and six enlisted men. The group made its way down Landstrasse-Haupstrasse, past the War Ministry and finally to Franz-Josefs-Kai. There they broke several windows and confronted officers not wearing republican cockades. Suddenly, they decided to seize Rossauer Barracks, where, after shots were fired and stones thrown, police finally dispersed the rowdy group.[3]

With such dubious offers of help, the new regime had to move quickly to control the situation. It became clear only too soon that what little remained of the Imperial Army was of no use to the provisional government. Circumstances had stripped officers of control over their men, and restoration of officers' authority was hopeless. Encouraging the men to form soldiers' councils to maintain order and discipline in the barracks proved popular but was not successful in holding the old army together. Many soldiers simply took an oath to the new state and rushed off to families they had not seen in years.[4]

Under the circumstances, governmental leaders were forced to adopt as a temporary expedient a paid, short-term voluntary army. This mercenary force, to be called the *Volkswehr,* was to serve as a provisional force until a more permanent solution could be found. In light of later polemics on the value of the *Volkswehr,* it may be well to emphasize that in November 1918 all parties—including the Social Democrats—agreed it was only a stop-gap measure.

The key personality in the creation of the *Volkswehr,* and the central figure in Austrian military affairs until the end of socialist rule in 1920, was Dr. Julius Deutsch. Born in 1884 in western Hungary (the Burgenland of the Austrian Republic), Deutsch had distinguished himself as an important socialist thinker by academic works on child labor and Austrian labor affairs. In 1915 he served as a reserve officer in the Austro-Hungarian artillery. He fought on the Rumanian front, saw action in Lithuania, and took part in the Battle of Caporetto at the end of 1917.[5] In January 1918 he was recalled from the Italian front to serve in the Imperial War Ministry as a trustee for the German-Austrian Labor Union Commission, an area of special concern following the January strikes. From his office in the War Ministry, Deutsch made contact in early 1918 with socialist soldiers in the Viennese barracks and succeeded in building a clandestine network of confidants. At first the contacts were somewhat loose, but in the summer of 1918 specific individuals were named to represent each body of troops and to maintain contact with the Social Democratic party through Deutsch.[6] These confidants, or trustees, served Deutsch well in November 1918 as the initial cadre of the *Volkswehr.*

The German Nationalist Josef Mayer was named secretary for military affairs by the Provisional Assembly on 30 October. Claiming the office of undersecretary, the Social Democrats nominated Deutsch for that position the following day. He was appointed to office on 3 November.[7] Deutsch had great latitude in organizational matters since Mayer concerned himself mainly with the administrative details of his office. As a leading Social Democrat, Deutsch intended to use the power he had to preserve the republican revolution and prevent the conservative reaction that Austrian socialists believed to be a more serious threat to the Republic than Bolshevism.

The Social Democrats' position, at least since 1911, had been that the best permanent solution to the military question would be a militia drawn from the whole population. It is difficult, however, to determine exactly what the socialist position was in the early days of November. Deutsch seemed to favor a voluntary army one moment, a militia the next. Above all, the socialists sought to prevent any future army's contribution to the cause of the expected conservative reaction. The socialists realized that much of the Austrian population was antisocialist, and feared that a militia drawn from the whole population could become a tool of the reaction. There was, therefore, considerable sympathy among socialists for a volunteer professional force dominated by the party.[8] Deutsch was successful in creating such a force, but in the process earned the enmity of the bourgeois parties, who soon came to see his *Volkswehr* as a Party Guard rather than a public arm of the state.

Deutsch kept recruiting for the *Volkswehr* firmly in Social Democratic hands from the beginning. During the evenings of 2 and 3 November, while across town the Emperor Karl and the high command were mishandling the Italian armistice, Deutsch gathered in his room a number of trustees from his clandestine network of soldiers, plus a few newly won officers and noncommissioned officers. He instructed them concerning the upcoming drive for the *Volkswehr*, emphasizing that the main goal was to build an organization capable of keeping order. If not done, "reactionary regular troops" would restore order and at the same time "destroy the revolution."[9]

As the guns fell silent in Italy, the new government in Vienna began its drive to build a new army. All the newspapers carried a State Council proclamation that recruiting for the *Volkswehr* would begin Monday, 4 November. Those registering for admittance to the *Volkswehr* were released from earlier military commitments, but could continue to serve in previous specialties and to wear medals earned for bravery in the Austro-Hungarian army. Once law and order were assured and a permanent solution to the military question found, all *Volkswehr* volunteers would be free to resign; until that time, duration of service would be three months, with provision for renewed enlistment. Only physically fit former soldiers of the Habsburg army were to be admitted, with pay of six crowns daily and three meals. Some squad leaders were to receive a bonus of an extra crown per day. Organized into battalions of three companies each, the *Volkswehr* was to rest upon a democratic foundation. The army's officers would be observed and supervised by soldiers' councils. Discipline was to rest ultimately with the "solidarity and sense of duty" of the *Volkswehr* men themselves.[10]

Response to the call for *Volkswehr* volunteers was disappoint-
ing. Workers in particular, who had had quite enough of soldier-
ing, resented the call to arms. The provisional government
continued to explore any possible ideas to control disorder.
Reflecting their hope in *Anschluss,* the German Nationalists
called for help from Mackensen's army retreating from
Rumania. However, the armistice signed on 3 November provided that German troops were to evacuate Austro-Hungarian
territory within fifteen days, so such a plan held little promise.[11]
Friedrich Funder, Christian Social editor of the *Reichspost,*
claims that for a brief time the provisional government tried to
maintain order using some 56,000 Rumanian troops who were in
good condition and well disciplined under Dr. Maniu, former
artillery officer in the Habsburg army. Funder's contention that
Deutsch "gave Maniu command of the city" is certainly an exag-
geration, but the incident underscores the chaotic conditions
prevailing in the city at war's end and the need for a force to
maintain order.[12] Diplomats to Vienna from neutral countries
agreed on 11 November 1918 to send appeals to the Entente and
the United States asking that the Allies occupy Vienna in order
to secure stability and order.[13]

Meanwhile, Deutsch proceeded vigorously to create a new
army that would appeal to Social Democratic instincts. On 9
November, the Ministry for Military Affairs issued guidelines for
building the *Volkswehr.* The purpose of the new army was
defined: to maintain order, to protect personal security, to guard
newly won freedom, and to help "insure a bright future."[14] The
Ministry for Military Affairs was designated as the supreme authority, and was to receive reports on all *Volkswehr* activity, the
names of leaders, and the locations of battalions. The Ministry
for Military Affairs would nominate and promote commanders,
and confirm existing commanders. A Supreme Commander of
the Armed Forces of German-Austria would exercise authority
for the ministry, which came ultimately under the jurisdiction of
the State Council. Nominated by Karl Seitz, Field Marshal
Adolf von Boog was named on 7 November to the position of
supreme commander.[15]

The official order creating the *Volkswehr* was issued on 15
November 1918.[16] The tactical unit of the *Volkswehr* was the
battalion, a complete supply and administrative unit whose commander was to be an officer. His staff was to include one adjutant
(also an officer), a doctor, a quartermaster, five clerks, three

messengers, and a paymaster. The battalion would consist of three companies in turn composed of three platoons. The companies were commanded by an officer with a staff consisting of a bugler, two cooks, and two medical corpsmen. The platoons were led by either an officer or a noncommissioned officer, and included about forty enlisted men. These plans anticipated battalions would number about 400 men. Some battalions could include four or five companies, however, so battalions exceeding 400 men were easily possible.[17]

Every company was to elect freely a trustee *(Vertrauens-mann)* to assist in administering the battalion. The pay office, clearly an important element in the mercenary *Volkswehr,* included one company commander, the battalion paymaster, and one trustee selected by the men of the battalion. To complicate matters further, there were soldiers' councils. The Ministry for Military Affairs promised in early November that the State Council would soon promulgate legislation securing the authority of the soldiers' councils to help in maintaining unity and enforcing the rights and duties of the *Volkswehr* men.[18]

Soldiers' councils were part of the *Volkswehr* from the beginning. In fact, just as they had done in Germany, soldiers' councils—patterned after the Bolshevik soldiers' soviets—had sprung up in units of the Habsburg army in October and November 1918. The councils were not the creation of the Social Democratic Party, but the socialists were quick to embrace them and bring them within the orbit of Social Democratic influence. Deutsch hoped soldiers' councils in the *Volkswehr* would help discipline and order, but he also saw them as a political tool to watch over the suspect officer corps, which he considered lukewarm at best in its support of the republic. By gaining control of the soldiers' councils through Social Democratic trustees, Deutsch sought both to improve discipline in the ranks and to guard against a conservative reaction.[19] Deutsch's nominal supervisor, Secretary Mayer, was less enthusiastic about the soldiers' councils than his socialist undersecretary. Reflecting bourgeois suspicions of a Bolshevik-inspired innovation, Mayer addressed a group calling itself the German-Austrian Soldiers' Council on 31 October and expressed his opinion that soldiers' councils were only a temporary expedient.[20] Whatever their future, though, there was little doubt as to their popularity with the soldiers in the early weeks of the republic. By 9 November, according to the socialist *Arbeiter Zeitung,* 300 such councils had been formed.[21]

Making virtue out of necessity, the provisional government incorporated the soldiers' councils into the hierarchy of the *Volkswehr* and even the Ministry for Military Affairs itself. Procedures were spelled out for electing the councils, and an executive committee of the soldiers' councils maintained close contact with the Ministry for Military Affairs in Vienna.[22] This institutionalization of originally spontaneous soldiers' councils became a source of great conflict between the Social Democrats and the other political parties in 1919 and 1920. As the soldiers' councils took on a definite Social Democratic complexion, the attitude of the bourgeois parties hardened against them.

Partisan struggle for influence in the military forces of the Austrian Republic was fought under the guise of the issue of discipline. Social Democrats argued that soldiers' councils were necessary to restore discipline, because officers' authority had been broken with the collapse of the old army; antisocialists, on the other hand, maintained that officers' authority had been undermined by soldiers' councils and should be restored immediately in order to curb disorderly Bolshevik elements in the ranks. Arguments and polemics in the political press over the status of the officer corps and the role of soldiers' councils reflected the predominance of bourgeois (sometimes monarchist) sympathies in the former, and socialist (sometimes Bolshevik) influence in the latter.

Although some officers had socialist and republican leanings, most former Habsburg officers who entered the *Volkswehr* were considered "unpolitical."[23] The Habsburg officer corps had always been ideally unpolitical, committed only to the monarch. After the monarchy's collapse, a good number of these capable servants offered their services to the new republic and dedicated themselves to "order." Eight *Volkswehr* regional commanders were selected on 13 November, most of whom were regular officers in the Habsburg army.[24] In addition to von Boog, named supreme commander, a number of leading figures from the old army served in Deutsch's provisional force. Steinböck lists sixteen members of the prestigious Maria Theresia Order who served in the *Volkswehr.*[25]

Nonetheless, the *Volkswehr* could hardly absorb the whole professional officer corps from the old army. In early December, the German Nationalist Teufel suggested forming *Volkswehr* units consisting entirely of officers in order to solve the problem of surplus officers. Deutsch fought the idea, arguing that officers would find it difficult to do enlisted work.[26] His real objection, of course, was distrust of the officers' loyalty to the revolution. In any case, Teufel's suggestion had little chance of success, for many officers refused to serve under conditions prevailing in the *Volkswehr.* In addition to the system of soldiers' councils, potential applicants were discouraged by rumors circulated by officers' associations. One persistent rumor, never borne out by later developments, was that officers serving in the *Volkswehr* would have difficulty gaining entrance into the "real" army of German-Austria when the time came.[27] Other rumors in early December of a pogrom against all officers, intended by the *Volkswehr* rank and file, compelled organizations representing officers' interests to express concern to the Ministry for Military Affairs.[28]

In spite of a surplus of officers in German-Austria in 1918, because many were unwilling to serve or were unwanted by virtue of monarchist loyalties, the *Volkswehr* experienced a severe shortage of junior officers. Deutsch resorted to filling positions by commissioning lieutenants from the *Volkswehr* ranks. On 20 November, Deutsch named twelve "*Volkswehr* lieutenants," his first effort at gaining a foothold for the Social Democrats in the new officer corps.[29] The commissioning of *Volkswehr* lieutenants was a bitter pill for older officers to swallow, especially those not in active service, living miserably on pensions paid in greatly devalued Austrian currency.

Deutsch's efforts to recruit soldiers for the *Volkswehr* met with increasing success in late November. The end of the war had brought industrial activity to an abrupt halt in Austria. Unemployment very quickly became a severe problem for the government, but it did encourage men from all classes of society to join the *Volkswehr.* Enlistment soared in December. Desperate economic conditions compelled thousands to join, where they received not only steady pay and regular meals, but a privileged position in the new society. As early as mid-November, *Volkswehr* men had been searching houses for unauthorized hoarding of coal or food, and preemptively seized whatever they judged to be in excess of permitted amounts.[30] Formerly humble day laborers and conscripts in the emperor's army found themselves controlling distribution of scant food supplies to all

Vienna, including the once high-and-mighty middle classes and the aristocracy. It is little wonder that the new elite committed excesses. Most *Volkswehr* recruits were unemployed industrial workers, and even Otto Bauer, left-wing Social Democrat, had to admit they were politically untrained and had been "bestialized" by the war.[31]

It was a constant struggle for Deutsch to secure control over the *Volkswehr;* despite the ministry's authority in theory, in practice the *Volkswehr* at the unit level took on a life of its own. In some cases, unit commanders earned the respect of their men; in other instances, soldiers' councils were the dominant authority. Some units obeyed orders and performed duties in a well-disciplined manner, others took the law into their own hands, and a considerable number advocated "completing" the revolution by violence in order to establish a dictatorship of the proletariat. It was this noisy Bolshevik element, threatening disruption from the Left, that proved more dangerous to Deutsch than the much-talked-about conservative reaction.

The Communist Red Guard, formed under a certain Leo Rothziegel in the early days of the revolution, was a continual source of trouble in the first months of the republic. Deutsch incorporated the Red Guard into the *Volkswehr,* which permitted him to exercise some control over disruptive elements without publicly disavowing their revolutionary idealism. By neutralizing the Red Guard behind a smoke screen of rhetoric directed against the presumed threats of conservative reaction from the Right, Deutsch may have performed his greatest service to the Republic.[32] Even critics of the "lawless" *Volkswehr* grudgingly admitted that Deutsch's tactic against the Red Guard eventually succeeded.[33]

But that success did not come without a struggle. On 11 November, Red Guard members residing in the Stifts Barracks *(Stiftskaserne)*—the main Communist stronghold under the leadership of the former journalist and reserve lieutenant Egon Kisch—marched into Deutsch's office and demanded to occupy Schönbrunn Palace, where the emperor and his family still resided. Deutsch suggested instead that the Red Guard "seize" the military command building, held only by a handful of elderly officers from the old army. After the operation, Deutsch inspected Lieutenant Kisch's victorious battalion drawn up in front of its prize. After solemn speeches and band music, the infamous battalion returned to its barracks.[34] On the same day,

Deutsch relieved Kisch of command. His replacement was Captain Dr. Josef Frey, a reserve officer in the war and an apparently trustworthy Social Democrat on the editorial staff of the *Arbeiter Zeitung.*[35]

The next day the comic opera became more serious. The occasion was nothing less than the birthday of the republic. Representatives of the Provisional National Assembly announced the new republic of German-Austria on the ramp of the Parliament building. Members of the Red Guard, through their soldiers' council, had promised to remain orderly for the occasion, and to parade without ammunition. Unfortunately they were successful in resisting the leadership of Captain Frey; the radical Lieutenant Kisch was left in charge of the unit. During the ceremonies, the Red Guardsmen suddenly stormed the Parliament building amid wild shooting. The crowd dispersed quickly and the building was secured by locking the doors from within, but some people were killed and many injured in the mêlée. No one will ever know for sure what sparked the incident, but there was widespread belief at the time that the Red Guard intended to take over the new government by a Communist *Putsch.*[36]

In December the disruptive Red Guard battalion was split in two, with more reliable men forming Battalion Forty under Captain Frey. A smaller number of suspect soldiers made up the infamous Battalion Forty-One, which was limited in size and closely monitored by the Ministry for Military Affairs and moderate figures in the Executive Committee of the soldiers' councils. By the end of 1918 the situation was at least temporarily under control, but tense. Lieutenant Kisch and his followers still represented a threat to peace and stability.[37]

Communist agitators were not Deutsch's only problem. Chaotic conditions throughout Austria as the old army "demobilized" posed a severe problem for the Ministry of Military Affairs. In some cases, men joining the *Volkswehr* considered their membership in the new army a license to plunder and steal with impunity. Frau Eisenmenger records an incident on 27 November when *Volkswehr* men broke into a slaughterhouse, killing livestock and taking for themselves precious fresh meat, some of which they traded for Frau Eisenmenger's rare supply of tobacco. When apprised of the meat's origin, she remarked, "A pretty business—and now we may all be sent to prison." Replied her servant girl, "Why, gnä Frau? They never touch the *Volkswehr* men; they can do what they like."[38] The government was aware of the problem, but quite helpless to police the *Volkswehr* aside from urging that responsible individuals within the *Volkswehr* exercise control over undisciplined members, as a directive from the Ministry for Military Affairs attests.

> In view of the massive movement of the Imperial and Royal Army home, and in view of the severe condition of the new state's finances and material wealth, the unregulated distribution of allowances and pay and the surrender of food rations and other supplies can no longer be tolerated.
> All *Volkswehr* commanders, in cooperation with their Soldiers' Councils, in whose interest the end of disorder can be shown to be, must redouble efforts to prevent plundering of public property. If necessary, severe punishment may be meted out. Control over distribution of materials . . . to *Volkswehr* members must be tightened.[39]

It is to the credit of hundreds of dedicated individuals who spoke out publicly in meetings of the soldiers' councils and workers' councils that a certain semblance of discipline and order was imposed upon the *Volkswehr*. Bauer argues that the hardest battles between Social Democrats and Communists were fought in "discussions within the Soldiers' Councils."[40] Particularly in Vienna, where soldiers' councils and their executive committees were considered full partners in the supervision of the *Volkswehr,* soldiers' councils eventually served a "useful and efficient" role in restoring discipline and eliminating "bad elements" from the *Volkswehr.*[41]

At the end of December, the government stopped recruiting for the *Volkswehr* in view of the great expense and the desperate condition of Austrian finances. Excluding those recruited for the *Volkswehr* in "German-Bohemia" and the Sudetenland, on 31 December 1918, the *Volkswehr* numbered somewhat more than 58,000. Some 16- to 17,000 of those were in Vienna; Lower Austria (including Vienna in 1918) accounted for nearly 34,000—well over half the country's total. Upper Austria, Styria, and Carinthia accounted for one-third the total with almost 19,000, leaving only slightly more than 5,000 troops distributed in the western provinces of Salzburg, the Tyrol, and Vorarlberg.[42]

Carsten claims that by the end of 1918, the Viennese *Volkswehr* had become a "fairly efficient and disciplined force," consisting of eighty-eight infantry companies, eight machine gun companies, and five batteries with twenty pieces of artillery.[43]

Professor Archibald Coolidge formed a similar favorable opinion upon his arrival in Vienna in early January to observe conditions in Austria on behalf of the American Commission to Negotiate Peace. "Authorities" in Vienna told Coolidge they were proud of the rapid and successful "demobilization" of the old army, and the relative quiet in Vienna, especially as compared with Berlin, Warsaw, or Budapest. They expressed to Coolidge their confidence in the *Volkswehr,* ". . . made up of workmen of the better class and whose councils of soldiers have so far been helpful to them."[44]

Coolidge, however, formed a rather different impression of the *Volkswehr* after he had been in Vienna several weeks and had observed conditions firsthand.

> The *Volkswehr* . . . for the most part appear as weak and emaciated a body of so-called troops as one can well imagine. The city police on the other hand are large, fine-looking men. The contrast is striking.[45]

Coolidge went on to say that Austria suffered from "lack of a trust-worthy armed force," and that a few thousand determined men could control the city. Only the police would oppose them, he said, for "the *Volkswehr* would be on the side of the mob."[46]

Coolidge's skeptical view of the *Volkswehr* and his favorable impression of the police in Vienna were shared by other foreign observers and by middle-class Austrians.

> Here in Vienna the labour leaders on the whole have the masses well in hand. Attempted revolts by the Vienna Communists are, thank Heaven, only passing episodes. This comparative security of life and property in Vienna is mainly due to the efforts of the Viennese police under Police-President Schober, who have thereby earned the lasting gratitude of the citizens of Vienna. The Viennese police remained almost entirely unaffected by the poison of party politics and were constantly faced with the difficult task of quelling outbreaks of party feelings and rendering them innocuous.[47]

Conservative and bourgeois groups (the two are not synonymous) in Austria generally favored strengthening the police and gendarmerie as a counterbalance to the socialist *Volkswehr.* The Christian Social *Reichspost* declared public support for a strengthened gendarmerie to provide security for Austria rather than a military force.[48] Police forces fell under the Ministry of Interior, which the Christian Socials had successfully claimed as their preserve. Dr. Heinrich Mataja, secretary of interor in the provisional government, succeeded in raising the total strength of the Viennese police to 7,800 men in 1918 by adding to the City Protection Guard *(Stadtschutzwache).* His early efforts to counter the socialist strength of the *Volkswehr,* however, met with mixed success, since the police ranks were fleshed out by drawing upon the "better elements" from the *Volkswehr,* and soldiers' councils were soon formed by soldiers assigned to the City Protection Guard.[49]

The key personality in the evolution of the police and the gendarmerie in Austria was Johannes Schober, who had been the capable Vienna police chief under the Habsburgs. Born in 1874 in Perg, a small town in Upper Austria, Schober was one of many children in a middle-class civil service family. Young Johannes performed well enough as a student at the Gymnasium in Linz to go on to the University of Vienna in 1894. His university performance was average, but he proved himself a capable and energetic bureaucrat in the Police Administration after completing university studies in 1898. He rose quickly through the ranks to become director of state police in 1913. His services to two emperors in Vienna during the war led to his elevation to the position of police-president in June 1918.[50] In 1918 he represented that typical hard-working Habsburg bureaucrat whose services were welcomed by the new regime.[51]

There is little doubt that in Vienna the police played a more important role than did the *Volkswehr* when force was required to quell disturbances. The *Volkswehr* served well to consume the energies of that class of people most inclined to disorder; the *Volkswehr* men busied themselves tracking down imaginary monarchist plots, searching middle-class homes for unauthorized hoarding of coal or food, and controlling food distribution in Vienna. The steady pay and many privileges and advantages afforded *Volkswehr* men gave them a stake in the status quo. But when violence did break out and disorder threatened, the police were usually the more reliable force. In fact, not infrequently, undisciplined elements of the *Volkswehr* were the cause of disorder and were brought to heel by the police. There is danger, however, in making simple generalizations about the *Volkswehr.* It was a diverse, loosely controlled organization containing all kinds of personalities. On numerous

occasions, *Volkswehr* units proved that—if they wanted to—
they, like the police, could control disorder by applying force.

The chief characteristic distinguishing the *Volkswehr* from the
police—aside from socialist sympathies in the former and a general orientation toward the Christian Social Party in the latter—
was that the police were well disciplined under Schober's firm
control while Deutsch had to depend upon persuasion and the
force of argument to keep the *Volkswehr* in line. A measure of
the government's distrust in its own creation was the order forbidding *Volkswehr* men to carry weapons from 9 February until 6
March 1919, during the election and formation of the Constituent
Assembly.[52] Not even Social Democrats claimed that the Ministry for Military Affairs had full control over the *Volkswehr*. However, they generally argued that the *Volkswehr* posed no threat to
civil peace and security.[53]

That the *Volkswehr* exercised a modicum of self-restraint was
owed to a number of circumstances, not the least of which was
the strength of character shown by Deutsch and other leading
"Austro-Marxists." They, in turn, had help from an unexpected
quarter. The civil war in Hungary led hundreds of the more
radical *Volkswehr* and Red Guard members, including Leo Rothziegel, to leave Vienna in March to fight for the Soviet regime in
Hungary. Rothziegel died in Hungary. About the same time, the
volatile Egon Kisch retired from participation in Red Guard activities in order to devote full time to the radical independent
newspaper, *Der Neue Tag*.[54] Pressing food shortages gave the
moderate Social Democratic leaders a most powerful argument:
Austrian socialists must show restraint or the Entente would
stop food shipments to the helpless country.[55] But ultimately, the
most profound threat to the *Volkswehr* came from the Austrian
countryside. The peasants resented the *Volkswehr* role in requi-
sitioning food and livestock, harbored deep distrust of Vienna
and its socialists, and could have brought the city to its knees if
Social Democracy had attempted to press its advantage too far.

Conditions in Vienna differed considerably from developments in the countryside and in provincial towns and
cities. In Vienna, Deutsch had some control over the *Volkswehr*,
even though it was effected by persuasion and constant cajoling;
outside Vienna, influence in *Volkswehr* units depended upon
local conditions and personalities. In Vienna, Social Democrats
led the *Volkswehr*, and unemployed industrial workers filled the
ranks; outside Vienna and industrial areas in Lower Austria, the

Volkswehr was not the exclusive preserve of the socialists, and was markedly less radical than Viennese battalions. In Vienna, aside from the potential Communist problem, the *Volkswehr* had only the police as a rival; in the provinces, *Volkswehr* units frequently quarreled with the gendarmerie, with locally formed citizen defense groups, and with armed peasants, not to mention the Czech army in Bohemia, Yugoslav irregulars in Carinthia and Southern Styria, and a fairly sizable Communist organization in Styrian industrial areas.

Just as in Vienna, soldiers' councils were formed in the provinces during November and December 1918. The Social Democrats hoped they would be able to use the councils and trusted confidants in the provinces to keep watch over conservative groups and to guard against the Communist threat.[56] However, the socialists proved to be less successful than they had hoped in dominating the *Volkswehr* outside the capital.

Provincial commanders were named on 15 November 1918 for Vienna and Lower Austria, Upper Austria, Styria, Carinthia, Tyrol, Salzburg, Vorarlberg, "German-Bohemia," and the Sudetenland.[57] The latter two areas were quickly cut off from Vienna. Czech troops had little difficulty in occupying them, despite clashes in the Sudetenland that resulted in bloodshed and loss of life.[58]

The *Volkswehr* in western Austria numbered no more than 6,000 at its peak.[59] Soldiers' councils played a small role in the west, and soon lost practically all influence. Officers regained authority quickly, especially in cases such as Salzburg, where local regiments of the old army were converted wholesale into *Volkswehr* battalions.[60] The Tyrol had long guarded its provincial autonomy, and in the first years of the republic made several attempts to break from Vienna. The *Volkswehr* in the Tyrol took orders from the Tyrolean National Council. Any orders from Vienna had to carry the stamp of provincial approval before being carried out.[61]

The *Volkswehr*'s strongest position was in the northeast, where Lower Austria (including Vienna in 1918) had the largest contingent, with nearly 34,000 soldiers and officers divided equally between Vienna and the surrounding countryside in the province. Upper Austria, with its industrial center and capital at Linz, ranked second in the republic with more than 9,000 men in *Volkswehr* uniforms. The *Volkswehr*'s chief activity in the northeastern provinces concerned control and day-to-day handling of food distribution. Eisenmenger's diary is filled with short episodes and vignettes that illustrate the *Volkswehr*'s predominance in controlling food requisition and distribution.[62] Serious food riots in Linz in February 1919 were quelled by *Volkswehr* units, but some *Volkswehr* men took an active part in the rioting.[63] Gendarmes in Linz had been unable to control the situation, but that was not always the case in rural areas. In the small town of Steyr, south of Linz, socialist attacks on a Christian Social newspaper office and looting at a nearby monastery revealed the tension and ill-feeling between the gendarmerie and the *Volkswehr*. The latter had prevented destruction of the newspaper offices but could not protect the monastery. The gendarmerie apprehended the looters and confiscated the spoils, but in so doing alienated the jealous *Volkswehr*, which took the side of the crowd. Shooting followed, and a number of people were killed and wounded.[64]

The *Volkswehr* role in food collection alienated peasants. The requisition of food and cattle from an unwilling peasantry quickly turned the peasants against the *Volkswehr* and encouraged antisocialist political movements.

> It happened occasionally that small bands of the *Volkswehr* went into the villages to requisition food. The peasants became furious with the *Volkswehr*. They had hoped that with the disappearance of the dynasty the hated army would also disappear. But there again was an army, and worse than the first, because it was in fact a Red Army, and a disorderly one.[65]

The development of the *Volkswehr* in the southeastern provinces of Styria and Carinthia proceeded under the shadow of conflict with neighboring nations. Carinthia was unique from the beginning of the republic, since Austrians of all political persuasion cooperated against the Yugoslav attack. Antagonism between the *Volkswehr* and other groups rarely flared into open conflict during the struggle against Yugoslavia in the Klagenfurt basin.[66]

Styria presents a picture in microcosm of Austria as a whole. Yugoslavs on the south posed a threat similar to that in Carinthia. Industrial centers and workers' organizations spawned a Communist threat not unlike that in Vienna. Clashes between peasants and socialists duplicated conditions in the northeast. Some local regiments of the old army were used as the nuclei for

Volkswehr units just as they were in the western provinces, although in larger southeastern towns the Social Democrats clearly dominated the *Volkswehr.*[67]

It seems clear that in 1918 the socialists alone in Austria were prepared for the monarchy's collapse and the demands for creating a new state in its place. Social Democratic success in gaining a predominant voice in the new government was matched by predominant influence in the new "people's army." The *Volkswehr* served the new republic well by controlling radical elements on the Left and forestalling possible reactionary movements from the Right. By defusing disruptive elements, the *Volkswehr* provided stability to the Austrian Revolution that other states—Hungary, for example—did not enjoy.

3

Between Left and Right

NONSOCIALISTS recovered quickly from their initial shock in November. Locally formed self-defense groups secured order in the countryside, while in Vienna the army question moved to center stage in Austrian politics. By spring 1919, conservative interests were developing alternatives to the socialist-dominated *Volkswehr*. At the same time, Communists on the radical Left mounted vicious attacks on the more moderate socialists.

The period from the first elections in republican Austria in February 1919 to the resignation of the first coalition government after the signing of the peace treaty in September, was, if anything, more tumultuous than the first hectic months of the republic. The election in February resulted in a fairly even split between the Social Democrats (seventy-two seats) and the Christian Socials (sixty-nine seats); the German Nationalists fell far behind, with only twenty-six seats. Despite ideological differences, the Social Democrats and the Christian Socials agreed to form a coalition government to promote the common good. The government formed on 15 March 1919 had Renner as its chancellor and the Christian Social peasant leader Jodok Fink, from Vorarlberg, as its vice chancellor. In an address to the newly elected Constituent National Assembly of German-Austria— successor to the Provisional Assembly—Renner warned that a government formed by two such different parties would need goodwill, wisdom, and "statesmanlike restraint" from all concerned.[1]

The new government would need all that and more. In addition to mounting economic distress and continuing food shortages, the threat of Bolshevism was never more serious than in

the spring and early summer of 1919. A Soviet Republic proclaimed in Hungary under Béla Kun just a week after the formation of the Austrian coalition government was followed two
weeks later (7 April) by the proclamation of a Soviet regime in
Bavaria. Both Communist regimes expected and encouraged a
Bolshevik revolution in Austria as the next step toward Soviet
revolutions throughout Europe.

In the meantime, and in reaction against the Bolshevik tide,
conservative groups marshalled a defense and mounted an attack against Marxism in Austria that frequently failed (perhaps
deliberately) to distinguish between Bolsheviks and moderate
Social Democrats. The governmental coalition was caught in the
middle of the crossfire: the Hungarian example inspired and excited Austrian workers just as peasants and conservative villa-
gers attacked socialism in all forms. Both the coalition parties
faced intense pressure from the extreme wings of their own organizations to end the unholy alliance with a political enemy.

Deutsch retained an important role in the coalition government. He replaced the German Nationalist Mayer as secretary
for military affairs; Deutsch's former position as undersecretary
was filled by Erwin Weiss, a Christian Social. Deutsch continued
his efforts to establish the *Volkswehr* as an effective force, but
gave increasing attention to finding a permanent solution to the
army question. As early as November 1918, steps had been
taken to create legislation defining an army for the republic. As a
step toward systematic military legislation, on 29 November the
cabinet had authorized Renner to present to the State Council a
draft outline of a basic law for the *Volkswehr* defining the rights
and duties of the *Volkswehr* men.[2] A provisional army law was
passed on 6 February 1919 but was expected to remain in force
only until a defense law could be passed that would formulate a
permanent solution, presumably a militia. The provisional law
provided for mandatory call-up of citizens between nineteen and
forty-two years of age in case voluntary recruiting for the
Volkswehr proved to be insufficient. Call-up was limited to
emergencies requiring troops for border defense, domestic disturbances, and natural disasters. It included many loopholes and
proved ineffective in Carinthia in May, when only seven companies and eight gun platoons could be raised. Even without the
loopholes, the law left at least two questions unanswered: what
would the Allied and Associated Powers dictate in Paris, and
would *Anschluss* bring incorporation into the German army?[3]

In early March, Deutsch clarified his position on the army question. He said that eventually Austria should have a militia, but the *Volkswehr* would remain until the Peace Treaty was formulated and the *Anschluss* question resolved.[4] Uncertainty about the future, however, did not prevent the writing of wide-ranging studies in the Ministry for Military Affairs on what sort of army would be best for Austria.[5]

Social Democratic success in the February elections served to enhance *Volkswehr* influence in March and April 1919. Socialism appeared to be the wave of the future; *Volkswehr* spokesmen grew even more confident of their position in Austria. The Ministry of Interior had gone to the socialists in the new coalition government, which raised the possibility of socialist control over the police. Police-President Schober told Coolidge in early April that the normally trustworthy police were showing signs of demoralization. They feared that, in the end, power would reside with the *Volkswehr,* and the police were afraid to antagonize the socialist body. Schober encouraged Coolidge to urge the Allies to intervene in order to strengthen the Austrian government's hand in its efforts to control the *Volkswehr.* Schober declared that in early March he could have disarmed the *Volkswehr,* but doubted his ability to do so in April. By May, he predicted, he could be "powerless."[6]

Coolidge agreed completely with Schober's position and warned his colleagues in Paris that the Austrian government was weak and unable to control its own supporters in the *Volkswehr.* The government, said Coolidge, was helpless against the excesses of the *Volkswehr,* which, if it chose, could turn the government out with little difficulty.[7] Conservatives in Austria had obviously found a powerful ally in their struggle against socialist domination of military force in Austria: representatives of the western powers, all of them nonsocialist, quite naturally empathized with conservative opinion in Austria. The impression of the *Volkswehr* extant in Paris was mistaken and distorted. A bulletin circulated at the Paris Peace Conference in early May called the *Volkswehr* a "national militia with Bolshevik tendencies" commanded by a "Communist named Adler."[8] In truth, of course, non-Bolsheviks made up the majority in the *Volkswehr,* and Adler was neither Communist nor commander of the *Volkswehr.*

The winter of 1919 brought severe food and fuel shortages in Vienna, coupled with high unemployment and rampaging inflation. According to Botz, by 1 May the number of unemployed in Vienna had reached 131,000—70 percent of the Austrian total. War veterans, and especially those disabled in the war, were embittered by their condition and questioned the efficacy of parliamentary democracy to improve their unfortunate lot. Communist propaganda was especially effective after February 1919 in capturing the imagination and raising the hopes of severely disadvantaged and embittered veterans of the Great War.[9]

The Soviet Republic established in Hungary in March provided a great psychological boost to Austrian Communists, as well as considerable sums of money and direct support and encouragement.[10] In early April the Austrian envoy in Budapest sent warnings to Vienna of Hungarian plans for a Communist *Putsch* in Austria sometime before 18 April; on 13 April he informed Vienna that leading Hungarian Communists—including Béla Kun himself—had just applied for visas to travel to Austria.[11] Vienna was astir with disturbing rumors of impending Communist coup attempts.[12]

Various Communist front organizations called for huge demonstrations to take place on 17 April, Holy Thursday. Various groups began to assemble in the morning, and by early afternoon coordinated demands at three different demonstrations called for going to the Parliament building and issuing an ultimatum to the government. By four o'clock, nearly 4,000 demonstrators had marched to the destination and demanded to see either Renner or Seitz. Both were in a cabinet meeting and not immediately available. Police barricades had been set up to keep the demonstrators from reaching the Parliament building, but governmental precautions failed to keep the crowd at bay. At 5:30 P.M., Deutsch and Schober agreed to summon all available men in their respective forces.[13]

Some demonstrators commandeered autos and drove to various barracks throughout the city encouraging *Volkswehr* battalions to join their cause. For a few moments, at least, the situation became critical at Stifts Barracks, located in central Vienna only a few minutes from the Parliament building. A group of young men attempted to equip themselves with arms from the barracks; for a time, the resident *Volkswehr* Battalion Nineteen remained passive. The *Volkswehr* men stirred themselves to roust the aggressors only after the intruders had disarmed police who attempted to stop the unauthorized action.[14]

By 5:30 the position of the police at the Parliament building had become untenable. The unruly crowd of unemployed and disabled veterans had been joined by a large number of armed members of the infamous *Volkswehr* Battalion Forty-one. Deutsch decided to call in reliable *Volkswehr* companies to assist the harried police, who had been unable to prevent the demonstrators from storming the Parliament building and there starting a fire in "faithful repetition of what the Red Guards had attempted in November, 1918."[15] Sometime after 7:00, shooting began; subsequently each side blamed the other for the commotion.[16] Schober called for the government to declare martial law, but Social Democratic objections prevailed. Between eight and nine o'clock that evening, reliable companies of *Volkswehr* men—including some reliable elements of Battalion Forty-one— arrived and relieved the weary police. The fresh *Volkswehr* troops were able to restore calm and extinguish the fire started in the Parliament building. The final toll counted five policemen killed, nine seriously wounded, twenty-seven otherwise hurt; ten soldiers and some twenty to thirty civilians were wounded. One civilian, an English woman, was killed.[17] Casualty figures suggest the police showed the restraint that they had been ordered to observe. The Holy Thursday incident came to an inglorious conclusion as darkness fell on the city and the agitators went home.

The poorly improvised Communist *Putsch* intensified the controversy surrounding the *Volkswehr.* Supporters of the *Volkswehr* defended its role in suppressing actions of "a few hundred hungry, ignorant, and despairing unemployed and disabled men."[18] Others, however, emphasized the participation of "hundreds" of *Volkswehr* men in the demonstrations and agitation and argued that even the *Volkswehr* units which eventually restored order were at best a "neutral" force.[19] The *Reichspost,* unofficial voice of the Christian Social Party, had high praise for the *Volkswehr* the morning after the incident. The usually critical newspaper singled out two companies of the Red Guard in particular, which "performed their duty in maintaining the peace in the same faultless fashion as other *Volkswehr* groups."[20] Nonetheless, the conservatives soon recovered from their brief flush of appreciation and resumed criticism of the *Volkswehr.*

The 17 April incident takes on significance for Central Europe quite beyond its seemingly trivial details and obviously poor preparation. Although the Communists tried (unsuccessfully) to deny responsibility for the half-hearted *Putsch* attempt, it was clearly a blow to Communist prestige.

The failure of the Austrian communists in mid-April 1919 was a decisive defeat for them as well as a debacle for the communist movement in Central Europe as a whole. It came only ten days after a new Soviet Bavarian Republic had been set up in Munich. . . . Pointing to the growing communist movement in Austria, [Pravda] prophesied: "Austria will now be seized by revolutionary fires from two ends; in the east from Hungary and in the west from Bavaria." In this critical hour the forward march of communism in Central Europe was halted in the streets of Vienna. . . . It was a major achievement, since communist expansionism for a brief historic moment had attained an aura of invincibility.[21]

The Holy Thursday *Putsch* attempt had two important results for the *Volkswehr*. The first was to enhance *Volkswehr* confidence and influence. Coolidge reported that the clearest result of the incident was to place the *Volkswehr* squarely "in the saddle." He suggested that the danger of immediate disturbances of a similar nature was diminished, but increased *Volkswehr* self-consciousness made the government helpless to resist *Volkswehr* demands.[22]

The second result of 17 April, a consequence of the *Volkswehr*'s increased standing, was that its enemies—on both the Left and on the Right—became more determined to undermine *Volkswehr* influence.[23] Demands made by the Italian Armistice Commission to reduce the size of the *Volkswehr* unwittingly assisted the Communists by giving them an issue upon which to base another more carefully orchestrated *Putsch* attempt in June.

The Italian Armistice Commission under General Roberto Segre had been an unwelcome and unpopular intruder in Vienna since its arrival in December 1918.[24] The Commission's duty was to insure that terms of the armistice signed on 3 November were carried out. The chief Italian demand was for railway rolling stock and coal, which had been removed by the retreating Habsburg armies in November.[25] Segre's demand in February 1919 for 100 locomotives and some 2,000 cars, plus several hundred tons of bridge materials, among other things, met strong Austrian objections. The Austrians argued that other successor states should contribute railway equiment *pro rata*. Austria appealed to "Italian fairness," expressing hope that Italy would not press a demand that could completely disrupt transportation of food into Vienna and lead to civil disorder.[26] Segre responded to the Austrian resistance by making good his threat to suspend one of four daily trains bringing food to Vienna from Trieste. Austrian compliance was quick. Segre, however, won few friends in Austria. His popularity was already low as a result of overzealous identification and removal from Vienna of art treasures that he claimed for Italy.[27]

The Armistice of Villa Guisti limited the future Austro-Hungarian army to twenty infantry divisions manned at peacetime strength levels. German-Austria, separated from Hungary, would be allowed the equivalent of thirty *Volkswehr* battalions. One of Segre's earliest directives in January 1919 was a call for the reduction of the bloated *Volkswehr*. Noting that the *Volkswehr* numbered about 56,000 soldiers (excluding officers), the Austrian Ministry for Military Affairs replied on 20 January that a reduction to 27,000 should be well under way by the first of February.[28] Little was done, however, in the following weeks. In fact, responding to an American inquiry on 17 March, Deutsch cited a somewhat larger figure of 57,000. He added that the high cost of the *Volkswehr* was hurting Austria; he hoped to reduce the *Volkswehr* to 27,000 very soon, but the high unemployment in Austria made quick reductions difficult if the "peaceful course of the new political order in Austria" were to be continued.[29]

In March the Austrian Ministry for Military Affairs made an unenthusiastic attempt to reduce *Volkswehr* numbers by offering a severance-pay bonus *(Kündigungsgeld)* of 150 crowns for private soldiers and 168 crowns for noncommissioned officers who left the *Volkswehr* with at least three months' service and a clean record.[30] Few had volunteered to leave when the problem regained Segre's attention in April.

Renewed Italian demands for *Volkswehr* reduction in early April prompted a curious response from the Austrians. They declared that the *Volkswehr* was not a military organization, but simply a force for the preservation of domestic order.[31] Undaunted, Segre informed Deutsch on 26 April that any battalions with fewer than 400 rifles should be immediately disbanded. Segre went on to direct that Austria should get rid of one-fourth the *Volkswehr* surplus every fortnight in May and June, thereby achieving a reduction to the allotted thirty battalions by 30 June 1919.[32]

On 4 May, Deutsch issued guidelines to *Volkswehr* commanders for reducing the *Volkswehr* to 20,000 men.[33] Infantry battalion strength was to be reduced from 41,300 to 12,000 by the end of June. The greatest impact would fall on Lower Austria, which was to drop from 25,000 to 7,200. Deutsch emphasized in his instructions, however, that 30 June was not an absolute deadline. He explained that the Italian note had directed reductions "as far as possible."[34] That provision proved to be more than adequate as a loophole; no significant reduction took place.

The Italian demand was hardly realistic under the circumstances. Given conditions in Austria, reduction of the *Volkswehr* was out of the question. Schober had already told Coolidge that any Entente pressure in that direction would have to be subtle in order not to provoke unnecessary resistance;[35] Segre was anything but subtle. The danger of Bolshevik regimes in Hungary and Bavaria, continued tension on the Yugoslav demarcation line, and the pressure of high unemployment made it virtually impossible for Deutsch to consider seriously any substantial *Volkswehr* reduction. Even before Deutsch had issued the guidelines for reduction, the soldiers' councils declared their unequivocal opposition to any reductions, and, for good measure, proclaimed their opposition to a militia, fearing it represented the beginnings of a bourgeois reaction.[36]

The violent end of the Red Bavarian regime on 2 May gave Communism another setback. It became even more urgent for the Hungarian Communists and their Austrian comrades to proclaim a Soviet republic in Vienna. The renewed Italian pressure for *Volkswehr* reduction played into the Communists' hands, since it gave them a popular issue to exploit. Detailed and careful plans were laid for a coup in June. Béla Kun sent Dr. Ernst Bettelheim to Vienna on 17 May, where he succeeded in passing himself off as an agent of the Communist International and gained control of the Austrian Communist Party.[37] The Entente demand for reductions in the *Volkswehr* assisted Bettelheim in his task by providing an issue against which the Communists could lead a united front, including Communists, socialist workers, and the rank and file in the *Volkswehr*. The widespread sympathy for the cause in Vienna led to almost daily demonstrations between 27 May and the fateful events of 15 June.[38]

Deutsch had persuaded the Entente, represented by Segre, to

delay the date for the first reduction until 15 June.[39] The Communists picked that day for a coup d'etat. Austrian socialists learned of the Communist plan for a 15 June *Putsch.* The Austrians urgently pleaded with the Entente to postpone the demand for a reduction in the *Volkswehr.* On 12 June, Foreign Minister Otto Bauer secured the Entente's agreement to delay the requirement.[40] The change in heart, however, came too late to stop Communist plans, although it did eliminate the grievance upon which their plans were based.

In a meeting of the Vienna Workers' Council on 13 June, Josef Frey and Friedrich Adler demanded that the Communists declare publicly their intentions for 15 June. Refusal to respond was taken as "answer enough" that they planned a *Putsch.*[41] Adler introduced a resolution prohibiting any demonstrations not sanctioned by the Workers' Council; it passed overwhelmingly. The Entente's concession on the *Volkswehr* issue had revived the temporarily sagging fortunes of the Social Democrats against the Communists within the councils and doomed the Communist *Putsch* plans to failure. The Workers' Council refused to sanction the demonstration planned for 15 June.

Schober pushed hard for preventive measures on the eve of the big day. The Social Democratic leadership vacillated on the question of arresting Communist leaders, but Deutsch had little hesitation in ordering *Volkswehr* units to occupy the Inner City. Armed representatives of the soldiers' councils confined *Volkswehr* Battalion Forty-one to its barracks; the threat of force kept the disruptive battalion from leaving to participate in any demonstrations. Without the approval of his fellow socialists, Secretary of Interior Eldersch finally authorized Schober to act. One hundred twenty-two Communist leaders were arrested by police during the night of 14–15 June, leaving the demonstrators without leaders on the following morning, when an angry crowd of five or six thousand men, women, and young people milled about on the *Ringstrasse* and finally concentrated in front of the *Rathaus.*[42] Eventually, the leaderless mob headed for the police station where the Communist leaders were held. Hopes of securing the prisoners' release were dashed by a cordon of police at the *Schottentor.* The demonstrators dispersed in the face of heavy police gun fire; the restraint shown by the police on 17 April was not repeated in June. No police or *Volkswehr* men were hurt on 15 June but twenty demonstrators were killed and eighty wounded before the day was done. Although the *Putsch* failed miserably, had it not been for the Entente's concession on *Volkswehr* reduction, for Schober's preemptive arrests, and for Deutsch's confinement of Battalion Forty-one by force, the result could have been much different.[43] Few argue that the Communists could have succeeded for long, considering the position of the western Allies and the peasants in the surrounding countryside, but most agree that the struggle could have led to great loss of life.[44]

Whereas *Volkswehr* prestige was enhanced by the Holy Thursday riot in April, the 15 June event raised the reputation of Schober and his police. The police-president was rightly given credit for the bold arrests of Communist leaders (released the next day), and police action was primarily responsible for dispersing the leaderless agitators. Bourgeois self-confidence surged after 15 June, as Schober received credit for being "Savior of the State."[45] With ill-concealed pique, Bauer denigrated the police role as he argued that the *Volkswehr* had saved the day.

> . . . The bourgeoisie tried later to twist the course of events so as to make it appear that the police had saved Vienna from communism. This is a foolish legend. On the 15th June it was not the police, but the Volkswehr which restored order.[46]

He continued the argument with a contention that *if* the *Volkswehr* had decided to support the *Putsch* attempt, the police would have been "completely impotent."[47] Upon close examination, this argument actually supports the conclusion that, despite hypothetical *Volkswehr* potential, the police broke up the crowd.

The Communists attempted a few more ill-starred adventures in Vienna throughout the summer.[48] By July, however, it was clear to everyone that Béla Kun's days in Hungary were numbered, and Communism no longer appeared to be the inevitable wave of the future. A weak Communist attempt to cause trouble on 10 August was typical. Three hundred armed members of the *Volkswehr* Battalion Forty-One planned to participate in a rally against the Christian Socials. The plan was thwarted when police armed with machine guns surrounded the barracks, forcing the soldiers to remain in the barracks.[49] By the end of August, Deutsch was finally able to disband the disruptive battalion, indicating that Communist strength had all but dissipated in Austria.

Deutsch had won the struggle against the Left, but in the

meantime the Right had gained confidence and momentum. The resurgence of police confidence checked the *Volkswehr* in Vienna, while in the countryside the *Volkswehr* faced growing *Heimwehr* and peasant power.[50]

Although the American representative in Vienna considered the peasants weak and disorganized, the British representative, Sir Thomas Cuninghame, considered the peasant threat to be real.[51] In early July Cuninghame issued one of the earliest warnings expressed by anyone in Austria that both peasants and proletariat should be disarmed.[52] The peasants had been organized by none other then Erwin Weiss, Deutsch's Christian Social undersecretary. In June 1919, Deutsch and Weiss formally agreed that Deutsch would represent the *Volkswehr* in the Ministry for Military Affairs, and Weiss would represent the so-called Peasants' League. By July, Weiss claimed the strength of the Peasants' League to be 84,000 in Lower Austria alone.[53]

On the eve of the peace negotiations in Paris, the *Volkswehr* and the police and gendarmerie were at a standoff. Schober served not only as police-president in Vienna, but also, as assistant to the undersecretary of interior, presided over the departments in that ministry for police and gendarmerie. In early 1919 Schober had sought to increase the numbers of gendarmerie and state police in provincial towns. Most local mayors were Christian Socials and welcomed the extension of police power. By May, however, the Social Democrats had won a good number of mayor's posts and opposed further introduction of police.[54] Relations between the gendarmerie and the *Volkswehr* remained tense throughout Austria; the socialists accused the gendarmes of showing favoritism to the rich, while defenders of the gendarmerie considered the *Volkswehr* an "asylum for the unemployed."[55]

The summer of 1919 brought little clarification to a situation that had become increasingly muddled throughout the spring. Socialists and nonsocialists alike grasped at any solution to the army question that appeared to offer some advantage over political foes. All paid lip-service to a vague sort of militia plan, but in practice the socialists were moving toward using the *Volkswehr* in some form as the basis of the new army. The Christian Socials preferred a strengthened police force and no army at all. None advocated a small, volunteer, long-term professional army. To their disappointment, that was precisely what the victors in the Great War were to decree from Paris.

4

Decision in Paris

In the peace settlement of 1919, just as in the War of 1914–18, the Western powers reserved their main concern for Germany. Decisions regarding Germany, frequently the result of considerable discussion and analysis, were applied rather mechanically to Germany's lesser allies. The disarmament of Austria and specifications for her new army provide a case in point. The Treaty of Versailles limited the size of the German army and specified conditions requiring long-term service in order to limit the number of young Germans who would receive military training. Similar terms were imposed on Austria, with little consideration for the peculiar Austrian situation. The Austrians were quick to call their long-term, highly paid, professional army a "mercenary" one.

Terms of the Versailles Treaty with Germany were barely completed when the Austrians were summoned, prematurely, to Paris. On 2 May 1919, the French Embassy sent an invitation from Clemenceau, president of the peace conference, to Austrian Foreign Minister Otto Bauer, calling upon the "Austrian Government" to form a peace delegation and send it to Saint Germain-en-Laye in order to "examine the peace conditions with the Allied and Associated Powers." On 9 May, Bauer replied that the National Assembly had conferred full power to represent "German-Austria" upon Chancellor Renner.[1] The delegation arrived at Saint Germain on 14 May, well before the victors were prepared to present the peace terms.

The question of military terms had been referred to the military representatives of the Supreme War Council in early May.[2] The military representatives discussed the problem at a meeting on 11 May. The principle of abolishing compulsory military service in Austria—which had been done in Germany's case—met with strong objections from French and Italian military representatives. Their main arguments centered on cost, the difficulty in finding enough volunteers, and the general principle that continental powers had found universal service preferable to a system of small, highly paid, standing armies. The British and American military representatives argued that the concept adopted for Germany should also be applied to other enemy countries, including Austria.[3] In the end, the military representatives agreed to refer the question to the Council of Four, where two separate proposals were presented on 15 May. The French-Italian proposal envisioned an army based on one-year, compulsory service, but which could include 8,000 enlisted or reengaged volunteers. Draftees were to be released from all further military service and obligations after one year. The British-American proposal, on the other hand, abolished universal compulsory service in favor of an army made up of long-term volunteers.[4]

In the council, Lloyd George defended the British proposal, explaining that a short-term army would result quickly in a large pool of fairly well-trained men who could then constitute a large army that in four or five years could be an "enormous" army. Clemenceau and Orlando agreed with Lloyd George's argument, which sealed the fate of the Austrian army. Orlando did mention that Italy itself could not operate without compulsory service, and he would object if *all* states in Europe were to be based on volunteer systems. However, since similar terms had been imposed on Germany, Orlando had no objection to doing the same thing to Austria. The question of cost was not raised in the discussion; the council approved the principle of a small, volunteer, long-term professional army for Austria.[5]

The principle of a small professional force was consistent, of course, with the one applied to Germany. The German settlement had sprung from fear of German military resurgence. The German limit of 100,000 men was complemented by insistence upon long-term volunteers. If Germany were allowed to train conscripts who would serve only a short time, a large pool of trained men would soon be created which could serve as the basis for a mass army sometime in the future.[6] The same argument was applied to tiny Austria, which could hardly be considered a military threat, the exaggerated fears of the Czechs notwithstanding.

The military representatives recommended to the Council of Four that the size of the Austrian army be fixed at 40,000. Clemenceau objected strenuously. He pointed out that Germany, with a population of sixty million, was limited to an army of only 100,000; why should Austria, with a population of less than seven million, get an army of 40,000? Lloyd George agreed that 40,000 might be excessive, but British Major General Sackville-West argued for the proposed figure, explaining that only 15-to 20,000 combatants could be gotten from a total of 40,000. After some discussion, the council agreed to return the matter to the military experts, who were to consider the size of armies surrounding Austria. Using the German figures as a guide, the experts were directed to calculate recommended limits for armies in Austria, Hungary, Czechoslovakia, Yugoslavia, Rumania, Poland, Bulgaria, and Greece.[7]

Figures were presented to the council on 23 May. Germany was allotted a proportionally smaller force than other countries, based on the consideration that Germany enjoyed an excellent system of transportation. Rumania and Poland were given proportionally higher estimates owing to the threat from Bolshevik Russia.[8] Wilson, Lloyd George, and Orlando expressed general agreement with the figures presented, but Clemenceau disagreed. He argued that armies for Czechoslovakia, Poland and Rumania should not be limited at all because they would be responsible for containing Germany in the west and for defense against Bolshevism in the east. Besides, after all Czechoslovakia and Yugoslavia "had suffered," they would not be "content" to be reduced in numbers. Lloyd George countered with his familiar argument that short-term conscription could greatly increase the number of trained men available to a country. He suggested that Czechoslovakia, for example, with 50,000 men in training each year, could have a force of half a million in twelve years. Such large numbers, he argued, would lead to instability in the area. Clemenceau, however, stood fast; the council postponed the question for future discussion.[9]

While the impatient Austrian delegation anxiously waited for negotiations to begin, the Drafting Committee and the Council of Four were struggling with the delicate but fundamental question of whether to regard Austria as a new state or an old state, heir to the Austro-Hungarian monarchy. Mr. Headlam-Morley, a British member of the Committee on New States and Experts, raised the issue of Austria's status in a meeting of the Council of Four on 26 May. Headlam-Morley noted that some parts of the draft treaty appeared to have been written under the assumption that Austria was a new state, other parts apparently drafted under the assumption that Austria was an old state—reduced in size, but in some sense the same Austria that had fought the war. He observed that it was "dangerous" to treat the new republic as possessing rights formerly belonging to the old empire. Lloyd George agreed, and proposed that the whole question be examined by the Drafting Committee, to whom the issue was referred in spite of French and Italian misgivings.[10]

Meanwhile, after waiting in Saint Germain for ten days without any significant communication from the peace conference, Renner sent a note to Clemenceau begging that negotiations be opened as soon as possible.[11] Although the Austrians were in consternation over the delay, minutes of meetings of the Council of Four in late May convey an atmosphere of haste and urgency. Members of the council were well aware that disturbances on Austria's undefined borders and the Bolshevik menace from Béla Kun in Hungary required that peace terms be stated as soon as possible. The council was displeased when on Monday, 26 May, the Drafting Committee reported that the treaty for Austria could not be completed before the following week. The next day, the Drafting Committee and the council agreed it would be possible to submit a draft treaty in proof to Austria on Friday, 30 May, with some clauses omitted.[12] The Austrians were told that the partial draft to be delivered on Friday would leave two questions reserved for further study: the strength of Austrian military forces to be maintained in the future, and the problem of reparations and public debt.[13] The council told the Drafting Committee to consider "with the least possible delay" the issue of whether Austria was an old state or a new state, and to "adopt whichever method proved most workable for the drafting of the Treaty."[14] One cannot escape the conclusion that simply getting the treaty completed was the council's overriding concern. However, there is no doubt that had the Drafting Committee concluded Austria was just another successor state, like Czechoslovakia, the council would have rejected the proposition. Clemenceau and Orlando in particular would have disapproved strongly.[15] Wilson agreed that Austria was not merely another successor state. He had suggested early that Austria be treated as a new state, but an enemy state (a somewhat illogical position).

Ultimately the Drafting Committee worked out phraseology that allowed the Allied and Associated Powers to avoid committing themselves on the precise relationship of republican Austria to the Dual Monarchy. This provided relief for the new Austria from economic claims or damages held against the whole of the monarchy, but Austria was still to be considered heir to the monarchy, an "enemy" state, and a defeated one.[16]

At a plenary session of the peace conference held the day before Austria was to get the partial draft in proof, delegates from Greece, Poland, Yugoslavia, Czechoslovakia, and Rumania asked the conference for a delay of forty-eight hours to allow examination of the proposed peace treaty with Austria.[17] As a result, the Austrian delegation did not receive a draft copy of the Treaty of Saint Germain until Monday, 2 June. At that time clauses pertaining to political relations with Italy, finances, reparations, the military, and clauses relating to the "Serbo-Croat, Slovene State" were not included.[18]

Upon receipt of the draft treaty, Renner delivered a speech (in French) to representatives of the Allied and Associated Powers, including Clemenceau himself. Renner objected to the principle that Austria should be treated as an enemy state, heir to the defeated empire. He argued that the Danubian monarchy had ceased to exist on 12 November 1918, leaving only eight nationalities who had formed their own independent states. Renner avoided a direct challenge to Clemenceau's stated position that merely changing the form of government or replacing leaders could not release a "nation" from its obligations. But Renner maintained that the onus of defeat, the "dreadful inheritance left us by the fallen Empire," should fall equally upon all the nations formed on the territory of the old monarchy. Renner's pleas had no effect; Clemenceau responded curtly that if there were no further observations to be made, the session was closed.[19] Renner and the Austrian delegation had had their first and last opportunity to speak directly to members of the Allied and Associated Powers. Future comments on the peace treaty and exchanges of views took place only in writing. Renner's frequent requests to address the council in person were always refused.

The debate on 4 June over the size of the Austrian army illustrates the advantage of direct access to the Council of Four and the attendant disadvantage of "enemy" states, such as Austria, denied all but written communication. On 4 June, Clemenceau maintained that it would be difficult to fix army sizes for eastern European states other than "enemy states." Lloyd George and Wilson reiterated their concern for limiting all armies in the area, and Wilson mentioned again the figure of 40,000 for Austria. Clemenceau insisted that 40,000 was too high. Lloyd George suggested a compromise figure of 30,000, to which all agreed. With that settled, the council agreed to extend an invitation to Paderewski of Poland, Beneš of Czechoslovakia, Bratianu of Rumania, Vesnitch of Yugoslavia, and Venizelos of Greece to meet with the council the following day and to accept the recommended figures for limiting their armies.[20]

Wilson addressed the various representatives on the next day, 5 June, explaining that figures for limiting their armies had been estimated by the military experts on the Supreme War Council. He added that the Council of Four wanted to defer action until after consulting representatives of the states involved. The representatives responded vigorously in speeches objecting to the principle of limiting armaments for "friendly Powers" in a peace settlement with "the enemy." All the speakers affirmed the desirability of limitation on armament, but suggested that the future League of Nations would be the appropriate locale for such a noble goal. They also referred to special problems, especially the threat from Bolshevik Russia, which compelled maintenance of larger military forces for the time being.[21]

After the speeches, Wilson confessed he was much impressed by the arguments, and "would have to think the whole matter over again."[22] Lloyd George agreed. Clemenceau and Orlando expressed their satisfaction with all that had transpired, and well they might have. The matter did not come up again. Austria, Bulgaria, and Hungary would have limitations imposed on the size of their armies; the "friendly" states of eastern Europe had no restrictions imposed.

The Austrians finally received a complete draft of the treaty, including all the military clauses, on 20 July. Renner and his delegation had until 6 August to submit comments on the treaty.[23] The Austrians had been genuinely shocked when they saw the partial draft on 2 June; the final version handed them on 20 July did little to relieve their distress. They objected to the idea that Austria be treated as heir to the monarchy; they objected to loss of territory, containing Germans, to Italy and Czechoslovakia;

they objected to the terms of financial reparations imposed on Austria; they objected to the stipulation that German-Austria remain separate from Germany; they objected to the victors forcing them to drop the nomenclature "German-Austria" in favor of "The Republic of Austria"; and they protested against the military terms imposed by the victors.[24]

The Austrians were particularly disturbed by the prohibition of universal military service.[25] Austria argued that in every continental nation, universal conscription was essential to the welfare and efficient governing of the state. But what was more significant, the impoverished Austrian republic could never afford the high cost of an army raised by means other than conscription. In discussions on 11 August, military representatives of the Supreme War Council examined the Austrian arguments. The French and Italian generals again advocated compulsory service for Austria, but recognized that the issue had been settled in principle by the Council of Four. The military representatives thereupon decided not to reopen the question and rejected the Austrian counter proposals and arguments.[26]

The Allies explained to the Austrian delegation that Austrian hopes for a militia system could not be accepted because it would give the republic the nucleus of an "important military force," a situation unacceptable to the Powers.

> [Despite the financial hardship] . . . the establishment of a military regime resting on obligatory service is absolutely contrary to the principle of the reduction of armaments which the Allied and Associated Powers have felt obliged to impose upon their former enemies as the only means capable of assuring world peace in the future.[27]

The final verdict, therefore, called for a long-term volunteer army limited to 30,000 men.

> Article 118: Within three months from the coming into force of the present Treaty the military forces of Austria shall be demobilised to the extent prescribed hereinafter.[28]
>
> Article 119: Universal compulsory military service shall be abolished in Austria. The Austrian Army shall in future only be constituted and recruited by means of voluntary enlistment.
>
> Article 120: The total number of military forces in the Austrian Army shall not exceed 30,000 men, including officers and

depot troops. . . . The Austrian Army shall be devoted exclusively to the maintenance of order within the territory of Austria, and to the control of her frontiers.

Article 122: All measures of mobilisation, or appertaining to mobilisation, are forbidden. . . .

Article 125: . . . Officers now serving who are retained in the Army must undertake the obligation to serve in it up to the age of 40 years at least. . . . Officers newly appointed must undertake to serve on the active list for 20 consecutive years at least. . . .

Article 126: The period of enlistment for non-commissioned officers and privates must be for a total period of not less than 12 consecutive years, including at least 6 years with the colours. . . .

In addition to specifications regarding conditions of service and limiting the size of the army, the treaty also limited the number of gendarmes, customs officers, foresters, and local police forces to the number of men employed in a similar capacity in 1913 within the boundaries of Austria as fixed by the Treaty of Saint Germain. At the suggestion of the Italian military representative, a clause was inserted forbidding any formation of troops not specifically authorized by the peace treaty. The British agreed quickly, since such a clause would seem to guarantee abolition of the *Volkswehr*.[29]

Article 124: Every formation of troops not included in the Tables annexed to this Section is forbidden. Such other formations as may exist in excess of the 30,000 effectives authorised shall be suppressed within the period laid down by Article 118 [within three months of ratification].

The victors specified their argument on the question of Austria's status in no uncertain terms in September. In the note accompanying final peace terms, the Western powers explained that it was "fundamentally erroneous" to argue that Austria should not be treated as an enemy. The Austrians were wrong in saying their republic ought not to bear in "any special manner" the burdens that would have been imposed upon the monarchy had it not ceased to exist. The Austrian people, the victors charged, together with the Hungarians, shared in "large measure" a responsibility for the "ills which Europe has suffered." The Habsburg dynasty could not bear sole responsibility for the war, for the Austrian people (that is, Germans in the old monarchy) supported their government "from beginning to end." In addition, the note went on, the Austrian delegation should be reminded that the German and Magyar elements predominated in the old monarchy, and the "system of domination" to which the Austrian people gave its support was "one of the most profound causes of the war."[30] The military terms imposed on Austria, as well as other more fundamental issues, were ultimately a direct result of the principle adopted by the peace conference that Austria represented the defeated heir to the Habsburg monarchy. Reluctantly, the Austrian delegation signed the Treaty of Saint Germain on 10 September 1919.

To insure Austrian compliance, the treaty called for the establishment of Inter-Allied Military Control Commissions. The commissions were to be organized to supervise Austria's execution of military, naval, and aeronautical clauses in the treaty.

Article 149: All the Military, Naval and Air Clauses contained in the present Treaty for the execution of which a time limit is prescribed shall be executed by Austria under the control of Inter-Allied Commissions specially appointed for this purpose by the Principal Allied and Associated Powers. . . .

Article 151: The Austrian Government must furnish to the Inter-Allied Commissions of Control all such information and documents as the latter may deem necessary. . . .

Article 152: The upkeep and cost of the Commissions of Control and the expense involved by their work shall be borne by Austria.

Detailed organizational planning in September and October 1919, following the threefold division indicated by the treaty, resulted in the formation of Inter-Allied Military, Naval, and Aeronautical Control Commissions. The permanent military representatives at Versailles—the Allied Military Committee under Marshal Foch—submitted proposals in early October to the Council of the Heads of Delegations, successor to the Council of Four. The new council approved plans that called for an Italian general to preside over the Military Control Commission, an Italian admiral to head the Naval Control Commission, and a French general to take charge of the Aeronautical Control Commission. The detailed scheme included creation of two subcommissions under each control commission, one for personnel matters, the other concerned with matériel and equipment.[31]

Article 153 of the Treaty of Saint Germain enjoined the Military Control Commission to supervise execution of the military clauses in the treaty pertaining to the formation of the Austrian army and the disposition of surplus and illegal army war matériel. The control commission was to "take delivery of arms, munitions, war material and plant intended for war construction . . . and to supervise the works of destruction, and rendering things useless" that were directed by the treaty. Article 156, in addition, called for modification of Austrian laws to meet the terms of the treaty.

The Military Control Commission included two subcommissions, one for matériel and equipment,[32] the other for personnel and army organization.[33] The council agreed that the first subcommission would be headed by an Italian general, the second by a French general.[34] It was only natural that Italians dominated in matters of matériel and equipment, a special Italian concern since the armistice signed on 3 November, which specified that considerable quantities of Habsburg military equipment and rolling stock be turned over to Italy. French interest in the size and limitation of the Austrian army, expressed frequently in council discussions, logically called for the selection of a French officer to supervise treaty clauses relative to army size and organization.

The Aeronautical Control Commission was charged with execution of aeronautical clauses in the treaty. The treaty permitted neither military nor naval air forces, and prohibited for six months the import, export, or manufacture of aircraft and related equipment. Therefore, the entire stock of Austrian aeronautical matériel devolved upon the victors. Articles 148 and 155 of the treaty explained this in some detail.

Article 148: On the coming into force of the present Treaty, all military and naval aeronautical material must be delivered by Austria and at her expense to the Principal Allied and Associated Powers. . . .

The material referred to above shall not be removed without special permission from the said Governments.

Article 155: It will be the special duty of the Aeronautical Inter-Allied Commission of Control to make an inventory of the aeronautical material which is actually in possession of the Austrian Government, to inspect aeroplane, balloon and motor manufactories, and factories producing arms, munitions and explosives capable of being used by aircraft, to visit all aerodromes, sheds, landing grounds, parks and depots which are not in Austrian territory, and to authorise where necessary a removal of material and to take delivery of such material.

The Austrian Government must furnish to the Aeronautical Inter-Allied Commission of Control all such information . . . which the Commission may consider necessary. . . .

The long delay in Entente ratification of the peace treaty postponed dispatch of the control commissions to Austria. Finally, in February 1920, the Conference of Ambassadors (successor to the Council of the Heads of Delegations) decided to send to Austria an advance echelon of the control commissions.[35] Since the treaty would become effective only after ratification by three of the principal powers, the control commissions needed Austrian permission to operate until France ratified the treaty (July 1920). The Austrians reluctantly agreed to the early arrival of an advance echelon in the belief that it would reduce the time required by the control commissions to complete their work.

Upon arrival in Vienna, members of the Inter-Allied Control Commissions immediately found themselves witness to a spirited political fight between the socialists and the conservatives in Austria concerning the nature of the new army demanded by the treaty, a fight that fundamentally turned on the issue of control over the army.

5

Echoes in Vienna

THE political battle in Austria for control of the army had
begun before the peace treaty reached final form in September
1919. General Hallier, head of the French Military Mission in
Austria, reported in early August on disagreements among Austrian factions over the organization of the new army and the
manner and degree to which the *Volkswehr* would be incorporated into the new organization. The Left, composed of Communists and "advanced Social Democrats" *(sociaux-démocrates
avancés),* wanted the *Volkswehr* to be maintained in the same
form. The Right—officers and noncommissioned officers of the
former Habsburg army, bourgeois parties, and some "provincial
Social Democrats"—inclined toward a completely new army to
be formed solely from former career officers and noncommissioned officers, excluding *Volkswehr* elements. Hallier had been
told that some 11,000 former officers and 7,000 noncommissioned officers were ready to enlist, even though the "greater
part" of them would have to serve as privates in such an army.[1]

The Austrian government hoped for a compromise solution,
an army retaining the best *Volkswehr* elements and incorporating
former career soldiers as well. Hallier proclaimed this compromise the only possible solution. The Left's solution would
clearly be unacceptable to conservative opinion; the solution of
the Right, in addition to alienating most Austrian socialists,
would require very high pay, and reactionary tendencies could
menace democracy. Hallier recommended that the Inter-Allied
Military Commissions be given jurisdiction over Austrian military reorganization in addition to supervisory responsibility over
delivery of arms, munitions, and war matériel. The French Gen-

eral suggested that the Austrian government would actually welcome Entente authority, since the government was almost "too feeble" to effect decisions on its own.[2]

In September, leading Social Democrats held hopes of retaining the *Volkswehr* as the foundation of the new army. On 15 September, Renner told Halstead, who had replaced Coolidge as head of the American Mission in Vienna, that the *Volkswehr* contained both "good elements" and "bad elements." The Austrian Chancellor had no plans to abolish the *Volkswehr*, but intended to reform it so that it could become a useful and dependable army.[3] On the same day, Deutsch told a gathering in Linz that the *Volkswehr* as a whole could be taken into the new army, but Deutsch predicted many *Volkswehr* members would not join under conditions of long service with no assurance of state support when their tour was completed.[4] By October, however, the Social Democrats had to admit a new army would be built to replace the *Volkswehr*. If nothing else, pressure from the provinces would force a change in the controversial name *Volkswehr* to a more traditional term, perhaps *Landwehr* or *Reichswehr*.[5]

The army problem was hardly the most pressing of those facing the Austrian government. Runaway inflation gave the government its most intractable difficulty. The finance minister, Joseph Schumpeter, had been unable to save the falling crown, which led to his repudiation by both parties.[6] Once the treaty was ratified on 17 October, the first coalition cabinet resigned, and according to plans negotiated by leading Christian Socials and Social Democrats, a second coalition formed immediately. The new coalition program called for eight Social Democrats, eight Christian Socials, and four professional civil servants (who were conservative and sympathetic to bourgeois interests) in a cabinet of thirteen secretaries and seven undersecretaries. The "apparent majority" of the conservative party brought a cry of opposition from radical elements, who claimed that socialist leaders had sold out to the middle class.[7] For a time, however, the attempts by both parties to govern in harmony succeeded in maintaining the uneasy political truce between socialists and bourgeoisie. An attempt to dampen the fires of provincial separatism was made by including representatives from Salzburg, Styria, and the Tyrol in the cabinet. The Tyrolese Christian Social Dr. Michael Mayr served as "State Secretary for the Preparation of a Constitution and Governmental Reform," a key position at a time when negotiations between parties over the constitutional issue concerning the extent of provincial autonomy threatened to split the coalition.

The coalition partners agreed to be equally responsible in the new government and to refrain from making labor and wage questions a political issue. The tasks before the government were formidable: effecting financial reform, drafting a constitution, establishing better relations with neighboring countries, feeding the population, and creating a new army. Any one of these problems would have strained political relations, so predictably, tension increased between the two ruling parties; the cautious optimism expressed by an American representative in Vienna described a situation that unfortunately proved to be short-lived.

The serious condition of the country has brought about a coalition of hostile political clements that nothing else could possibly have accomplished. The bright spot in the situation is that this coalition may go far to soften the hatred between the classes, at least between the classes as represented by the two large political parties.[8]

The coalition program, published in both the *Arbeiter Zeitung* and the *Reichspost,* called for a democratic, republican army. The emphasis on loyalty to republican principles, according to Jedlicka, reflected the socialists' demand for protection against a conservative reaction and a Habsburg restoration.[9] The new army was to be an army of the whole republic, and not that of a single party—an obvious reference to the *Volkswehr.* However, the additional proviso that soldiers would enjoy full citizens' rights, including participation in politics, doomed the hope for a nonpolitical army. Officers from the old Austro-Hungarian army would be selected for the new army, along with qualified *Volkswehr* lieutenants. For officers of the old army who did not join the new Federal Army, some sort of governmental employment was to be provided. Soldiers' councils were to be retained in the Federal Army, but would be prevented from infringing upon the powers of commanders. And reflecting the Christian Social concern that the army's ranks might be filled by unemployed socialists from "Red Vienna," soldiers were to serve only in their own provinces. Exceptions could be made if there were insufficient volunteers to fill the provincial quotas.

Conservative fears that the army would be predominantly socialist appeared justified in November and December. Peasants were even more reluctant to commit themselves to long-term service than were the workers. The prospect of an army composed entirely of socialists prompted the British commissioner in Vienna, Mr. F. O. Lindley, to suggest it might become necessary for the Entente to intervene. For the time being, however, London authorities ordered no interference in a matter they considered one of internal Austrian politics.[10] The fact was, however, that the Austrian army question was an international problem. The guidelines for building the army had been dictated in Paris. Had the matter truly been a question of Austrian internal politics, there would have been no long-term standing army. No doubt a militia system of some sort would have evolved and one suspects a *modus vivendi* between the existing *Volkswehr* and emerging *Heimwehr* could have developed. Instead, the Western powers forced Austria to fashion a professional army and pressed Austria to suppress and dissolve militialike paramilitary groups throughout the land.

Deutsch introduced an army bill on 14 January 1920, which followed the general outline of the coalition program published in October 1919. The compromise bill met with considerable disfavor in the National Assembly from bourgeois and peasant representatives, especially the German Nationalists, who declared their intention to vote against the bill. The proposed legislation specified no commander of the army in peacetime, which critics feared would give undue socialist coloring to the force. Even though soldiers' councils were abolished, nonsocialist opponents were not satisfied: the proposed bill called for trustees *(Vertrauensmänner)* to replace the soldiers' councils. The trustees would assist and represent the rank and file in matters relating to recruiting, discharge, feeding, leave, pay, housing, equipment, and training for future civil employment. Despite the explicit prohibition against trustees interferring in matters of command, opponents of the bill in the assembly—led by Mataja, former secretary of interior and champion of a strengthened gendarmerie instead of an army—insisted that the scope of trustee activity be more strictly curtailed. Critics also argued that political activity in the future army needed further limitation to achieve the stated objective of an army free from party politics. The proposed bill prohibited soldiers from participation in party politics while in active service and outlawed political meetings in barracks rooms. Spokesmen for nonsocialist interests wanted the ban on political activity to include barracks grounds and all buildings used by the army. The issue of discipline remained a point of controversy; opponents of the bill criticized the proposal to allow rank-and-file soldiers to sit on courts of discipline when officers or noncommissioned officers were on trial. Criticism of proposed recruiting procedures foreshadowed the importance that issue would have in the struggle to control the army. The nonsocialists, aware of their political majority in the provinces and overwhelming preponderance among the peasants, consequently were concerned that the terms of service would attract few peasants. Conservatives wanted guarantees that socialist workmen from industrial districts would not fill positions originally set aside for citizens from the provinces.[11]

Controversy over the army bill continued when the proposal was referred to committee on 19 January. The Christian Socials declared the forthcoming federal constitution would require an army law quite different from the bill submitted to the assembly. They argued that provincial authorities should have more influence and control, and more effective measures would be needed to prevent the army from becoming an instrument of a single political party, especially in light of the possibility that soldiers would be recruited solely from the towns.[12]

In early February the Christian Social Party gained a significant advantage in the army debate. Mataja was named reporter of the army bill in exchange for a corresponding concession to the socialists on a controversial capital tax bill. Mataja stated in committee debate on 13 February that the army bill could not prejudice the future local independence of provincial authorities, and the mutual mistrust surrounding the army bill in its original form required radical amendment to the bill. Mataja gave Deutsch credit for trying to create a nonpolitical force, but Mataja suggested "other forces" were intent on creating a socialist force. Referring to *Der freie Soldat,* official newspaper of the soldiers' councils, and to statements by Dr. Frey and others, Mataja charged that powerful groups sought to make the new Federal Army a "radical socialist party instrument."[13] The bill, finally resubmitted to the Committee for Army Affairs in late February, contained modifications of the original bill, in Cuninghame's words, ". . . so far-reaching that they amount to a new draft."[14]

Mataja's new bill called for an Army Administration Bureau in every province, which would control recruiting. The bureau would be directed by an officer appointed by the central government in Vienna in agreement with provincial authorities. Mataja's formula did not explicitly forbid importing recruits from other provinces, but by placing control of recruiting in the hands of local authorities, the danger of large scale importation of urban workers was eliminated. Furthermore, Mataja's bill forbade participation in party politics. Soldiers on duty were prohibited from attending political meetings. Soldiers would, of course, retain their right to vote, a right that superior officers had a duty to safeguard. Officers for the new army were to be chosen *only* from the ranks of ex-officers of the Habsburg army; officers serving in the *Volkswehr* were excluded under Mataja's scheme, except for certain reserve officers in special circumstances. *Volkswehr* officers could only claim positions as officer candidates, requiring additional training before commissioning.[15]

Needless to say, the details of Mataja's proposal generated great furor when publicized in Viennese newspapers on 27 February. Spokesmen for the soldiers' council declared the proposals were "quite beyond discussion," claiming that the *Volkswehr* would never allow an army law that subjected the men to the mercy of reactionary officers. The proclamation defiantly announced that the *Volkswehr* men would know how to prevent enforcement of unpopular provisions in the law and would not put down their arms until an army law was passed which guaranteed that the future army would not become an instrument of reaction. On the other hand, voices from the Right objected that Mataja's modifications did not go far enough. Spokesmen for the Tyrol, Salzburg, and Vorarlberg complained that the revised army bill still failed to safeguard sufficiently the prerogatives of the provinces to control their own units. As a result, a movement began to postpone passage of any army law until agreement was reached on the details of the federal law governing relations between the provinces and Vienna.[16]

A delay in passing the army law would have been to the advantage of those groups that advocated no army at all or at least a greatly strengthened gendarmerie and police force. These groups interpreted the Treaty of Saint Germain to allow increased numbers of gendarmerie or police as long as the army was correspondingly smaller than the 30,000 maximum. The Social Democrats, in contrast to this position and expecting to obtain a predominantly socialist force in Vienna and other industrial areas, interpreted the peace treaty as obliging Austria to maintain an army at full strength.[17]

The short-lived Kapp *Putsch* in Germany on 13 March, demonstrating the dangers of right-wing reaction, as well as the threat posed by an army divided against itself, forced the Austrian parties to compromise on the army bill and to pass it on 18 March 1920. The March army law reflected concessions from both sides. The Christian Socials allowed considerable freedom of action to the trustees, agreed to permit limited political activity by soldiers, and granted *Volkswehr* lieutenants the right to join the Federal Army. The Social Democrats also gave in on some points, especially on the matter of greater provincial control over army contingents, including complete integrity of provincial recruiting areas and prevention of personnel transfers from one province to another.[18]

Neither party considered the compromise bill satisfactory, and military experts pronounced the scheme unworkable in practice. The division of authority between the central government and the provinces included provisions that each province would promulgate service rules for its own contingent, and soldiers were to take an oath to uphold laws of both the central government and provincial laws. Until the constitutional question reached solution, serious potential for a conflict in the laws could paralyze the army.[19]

The army law of March 1920 did not solve the army question. Neither the nature of the new army nor its role in Austrian society and politics were finally decided by the compromise measure. Powerful conservative groups, frequently supported by Western powers and hoping for a strengthened gendarmerie and police force, did not consider the March army law to be the final word.[20]

The army law passed on 18 March was closely related to two other matters: provisions of retirement for surplus officers and dissolution of the *Volkswehr*. At the beginning of 1920, there were fewer than 2,000 officers serving in the *Volkswehr*, but as Deutsch noted in a budget debate on 19 January, the state continued to pay some 9,000 ex-officers of the old army. The dispute over pension and retirement benefits for ex-Habsburg officers was hardly less vigorous than the quarrel over the army bill. Under the old laws of the empire, an officer was entitled to a pension equivalent to 40 percent of his pay after serving ten years, rising 2 percent every year up to 100 percent upon completion of forty years' service. In view of Austria's financial plight, such generous terms could no longer prevail. The secretary for military affairs proposed to pension off all officers not chosen for service in the Federal Army who had at least nineteen years of service (including two years at the military academy). The financial ministry considered even these terms too liberal, and hoped to restrict pension payments to those officers who had served at least twenty-six years. The Christian Socials objected bitterly to the position taken by the finance ministry, and promised officers' organizations in March that the party would oppose the new scheme. In any case, it was clear to all that the issue of surplus officers was tied to the larger question of the army bill. When the Kapp *Putsch* forced a compromise on the bill, agreement was also reached concerning officer retirement. The Christian Socials essentially got their way; officers with between fourteen and twenty-four years of service could choose either a pension or a bonus.[21]

Dissolution of the *Volkswehr* was more complicated. The Social Democrats had recognized for several months that the *Volkswehr* must go, but sought to disband it in such a way that socialist influence would be enhanced in the new Federal Army. In January, Deutsch set the stage in a parliamentary debate, declaring that the unreliable element had been purged from the *Volkswehr*, that order and discipline had been restored, and the *Volkswehr* consisted only of "blameless, irreproachable and faultless men."[22] However, the socialists were quite aware that wholesale transformation of the *Volkswehr* into the new army of Saint Germain would never be possible. An army order in February attempted to reduce the size of the *Volkswehr* by offering a special bonus to those who left the force before 15 April and agreed to make no application to join the new army for two years thereafter.[23] Presumably, if all went according to plan, on 16 April the *Volkswehr* would consist only of men who wished to join the Federal Army.

Many officers and noncommissioned officers applied for admission to the Federal Army in March, but few private soldiers were interested. Expectations proved correct that long-term service would attract few peasants, but much to everyone's surprise, the new army did not appeal to socialists any more than it did to peasants. Echoing concern over the lack of socialist response, members of the soldiers' council of Vienna agreed on 24 March that "every endeavor" should be made to induce socialists to join the new army. Members comforted themselves by resolving that soldiers' councils would continue to control the command power of those officers recognized as monarchist. The representatives also called for the executive committee to organize a trades union for all "real republican" members of the new Federal Army. Such talk and threatening resolutions did little, of course, to allay fears of nonsocialists who had hoped to eradicate socialist influence from Austria's new army. In early April, Cuninghame observed that provincial authorities would prefer to maintain no force at all rather than fill quotas with socialists from Vienna and other industrial areas.[24]

A period of so-called "first recruiting" ran from 1 April to 31 April, handling career officers and noncommissioned officers from the Habsburg army and private soldiers who had served at least one year in the old army or the *Volkswehr*. Headed by ex-regular officers, army administration bureaus operated in each of the provinces, with three in Vienna.[25] The bureaus functioned side by side with provincial authorities, represented by an advisory committee, and with existing organs of the *Volkswehr*. At the end of April, the army administration bureaus were supposed to absorb the *Volkswehr* apparatus.[26]

The socialists persuaded the cabinet to postpone from 16 April until 30 April the last date for notification of discharge from the *Volkswehr*. The Social Democrats hoped to use the extra time to proselytize among new recruits. There was, however, little opportunity to do so. During the first half of April, neither Social Democratic hopes nor Christian Social fears were realized: only small numbers of *Volkswehr* men volunteered for transfer to the new army. In spite of the bonus offer, few made any effort to leave the *Volkswehr* or to enroll in the new Federal Army. In mid-April, the final deadline for dissolution of the *Volkswehr* was postponed once again, allowing Social Democrats an opportunity to mount an extensive propaganda campaign to recruit *Volkswehr* men for the new army.[27] Efforts finally paid off: by the end of April, rates of enlistment had improved. Nearly three-quarters of the *Volkswehr* in Lower Austria applied for admission to the Federal Army. All indications pointed to the new army becoming a tool of the Social Democratic Party.[28] Peasant response in the rural areas was, if anything, worse than expected. In Salzburg, for example, a mere 200 applications had been received by 29 April for 1,000 positions. All but fifteen of the 200 applications were socialist.[29]

The Federal Army was organized into mixed brigades whose strength reflected provincial capabilities. Six technical battalions were planned, owing to mountainous terrain dominating Austria and flooding problems caused by the Danube and its tributaries.[30] Initially, however, all men were to be enrolled in infantry battalions in order to have a substitute for the dissolving *Volkswehr.* Each province was allotted a quota of enlistment that could not be exceeded. Nearly half the total quota came from Vienna and Lower Austria. The First Brigade would be drawn from Vienna, Lower Austria, and the Burgenland; the Second Brigade from Vienna alone; the Third Brigade from Lower Austria; the Fourth Brigade from Upper Austria; the Fifth Brigade from Styria; and the Sixth Brigade from Carinthia (two battalions), Tyrol (two battalions), Salzburg (one battalion), and Vorarlberg (one battalion). At full strength, each brigade was generally authorized from five to eight infantry battalions, a cycle battalion, a cavalry squad, an artillery detachment, and one technical battalion.[31]

Progress in forming the army was slow throughout the summer, primarily owing to the tedious process of checking each applicant through the police before enlisting him in the Federal Army. In addition to this administrative difficulty, there was considerable resistance from provincial authorities who were unhappy with their small role in the new army scheme, and who often prevented recruiting officers from transmitting required papers for applicants to Vienna. Objections to recruiting for the Federal Army were so great in Carinthia and the Tyrol that some 1,000 *Volkswehr* men had to stay on until sufficient army recruits could be enlisted. By the end of June 1920, fewer than 14,000 men had been enlisted for an army that was to number 26,500 private soldiers. By the end of August, the situation had improved slightly, but provincial contingents other than Vienna and Lower Austria were still substantially below their quotas. On 31 August only 20,791 men were reported as enlisted to the Inter-Allied Military Control Commission. There was little difficulty, however, in filling quotas for officers and noncommissioned officers. The 1,500 officer positions and 2,000 noncommissioned officer slots were completely filled by 1 September 1920.[32]

Recruiting patterns contributed to a widening gulf between private soldiers, often socialist, and career officers and noncommissioned officers, generally conservative. The development of military trades unions contributed further to a politicized army.

The March army law granted soldiers permission to join associations and unions. On 1 May 1920 the Social Democrats organized the Military Union of Austria, open in theory to all soldiers, including officers, but in practice a socialist preserve, composed mostly of private soldiers. The Ministry for Military Affairs approved the trades union on the grounds that a similar organization already existed for officers—the Front Veterans Association *(Frontkämpfervereinigung)*.[33]

The struggle for control of the Federal Army was simply one part of a wider contest between political groups in Austria for dominance in the state. Mutual distrust encouraged both factions to pour energy into organizing and developing party guards outside the legal army. The spring and summer of 1920 brought para-military groups into public view and contributed significantly to strains in the coalition.

The long-expected breakdown of the ruling coalition occurred in June 1920. The issue over which the Social Democrats and Christian Socials split was a decree promulgated by Deutsch concerning soldiers' councils that demonstrated the importance of army control in Austrian politics.

> The red army was a bone of contention second to none between the Socialists and the other Austrian parties, and it was indeed largely on a quarrel over it that the former finally retired from the Government.[34]

The coalition of Social Democrats and Christian Socials that governed Austria from February 1919 until June 1920 stands as one of the most remarkable achievements of the Austrian revolution. The parties cooperated and compromised on a number of difficult issues that were beneficial in Austria's struggle for existence in the postwar period. In light of bitter party quarrels in the 1920s and 1930s, it is easy to forget that from March 1919 until March 1920, two men, who would later become bitter foes, cooperated and worked together for socialization of the Austrian economy. Otto Bauer served as president of the socialization commission, Ignaz Seipel as vice president. The end of the coalition in June 1920, long expected, marked the closing of a distinct period in Austrian political history.

Deutsch himself provided a good description of the Austrian political configuration in a conversation with Cuninghame on 2 June, shortly before the coalition break. Deutsch observed that the Social Democratic Party could be divided into three wings.

Bauer and Adler led the left wing; Renner and Seitz led the right wing; and Deutsch put himself in the center position. He also divided the Christian Social Party into three wings: the "moderate element," led by Weiskirchner, Fink, Hauser, and Stöckler with his peasants; the center, represented by Seipel; and the "extreme" wing led by Mataja. Deutsch agreed with Cuninghame that Kunschak, perhaps the leading Christian Social in the summer of 1920, pursued an inconsistent policy and could not be neatly classified. Deutsch concluded by noting that the chief threat to the coalition came from the right wing of the Christian Social Party and the left wing of the Social Democratic Party, both of which hoped to see the coalition end.[35]

Signs of trouble for the coalition had been visible throughout the spring in 1920. On 2 March Kunschak replaced Hauser as head of the Christian Social Party, leading to rumors that the Christian Social Party intended to commence a campaign against the coalition. At the same time, the left wing of the Social Democratic Party continued its pressure on party leaders to break with their conservative colleagues in the coalition. Renner argued in favor of continuing the coalition in a speech on 30 March, and on 14 April, at Bruck on the Mur, said that the present government needed to pass the Capital Tax Bill and agree on constitutional reform before elections were held in the autumn. Nevertheless, in early May there was talk of a scheme to replace the coalition with a "cabinet d'affaires," a ministry of functionaries not deeply committed to either party.[36]

The most troublesome issue between the parties was constitutional reform, tied to the difficult problem of determining the degree of latitude to be allowed the provinces in the Austrian federal system. The socialists advocated central control from Vienna, while conservative leaders and politicians in the provinces wanted the loosest possible association with "Red Vienna." The second issue was a Capital Tax Bill, which touched deep ideological differences between the parties. The third issue of significance was the army question, made only more volatile by socialist successess in recruiting for the Federal Army, the growing threat of private military organizations, and continuing efforts of the Christian Socials to strengthen the police and gendarmerie. Excesses of the remaining vestiges of the *Volkswehr* and increasingly vocal pronouncements by conservative officers' organizations raised the intensity of party polemics.

On 9 April a group of *Volkswehr* men forced their way into a

meeting of Austrian exofficers in the Officers' Club in Schwar-
zenberg-Platz in the mistaken belief that the meeting was
monarchist in sympathy. In fact, the meeting was held in behalf
of the National Union of German-Austrian Officers, with the
intent of passing a resolution in favor of *Anschluss.* Police were
required to break up the ensuing scuffle between the two groups
and eject the intruders. Later in the month, a group of socialist
workmen, denied access to a meeting of a bourgeois political
organization, sought help from a nearby *Volkswehr* battalion.
Against the orders of their commander, the *Volkswehr* unit
marched to the scene and surrounded police who were guarding
the meeting. Only when police reinforcements arrived were the
Volkswehr offenders driven off.[37]

Socialist excesses stimulated conservatives to continued efforts in developing the police and gendarmerie as a counter force
to the tainted *Volkswehr* and suspect Federal Army. In April,
Schober laid plans to phase out the City Protection Guard, composed of better *Volkswehr* elements, and replace it with an equal
number of regular police. Schober also wanted to retain 16,000
total police and gendarmerie, which exceeded Saint Germain
limits by 5,000, in exchange for a reduction in the Federal Army
to 25,000.

The proposal had enthusiastic support from high-ranking Allied representatives in Vienna. The British high commissioner
wrote to London in April urging accommodation to Schober's
scheme.

> The necessity for a national army for Austria has never been
> clear to me and I should have preferred, in the present im-
> poverished condition of the country, to have seen the whole
> thing dropped and a part of the money thus saved expended on
> improving conditions and increasing the numbers of Gendar-
> merie and Police. The Government are, however, bent on hav-
> ing a national army . . . probably . . . because they wish to
> have an armed force imbued with Socialist ideas. . . . I trust
> that . . . no hindrance will be put in the way of the Austrian
> Government increasing the Gendarmerie and Police provided
> they reduce the strength of the army correspondingly.[38]

Socialists, naturally, objected to conservative plans for the
police, and relations between Schober and the Social Democratic Party grew bitter in May after a socialist demonstration in
which speakers called for placing the state police under munici-

pal jurisdiction, a principle that Schober believed would destroy the police. Schober viewed the comments as critical of his administration and as sanctioned by leaders of the socialist party. Matters became only more inflamed by polemics in the press and mutual denunciations throughout the month of May.[39]

In early June, the ruling coalition was clearly in trouble. Great differences remained that separated the parties. Disagreements on the Capital Tax Bill led to attacks upon the government by the *Reichspost,* semiofficial newspaper of the Christian Socials, which drove the center of the Social Democratic Party closer to the left wing, which wanted to end the coalition. Despite speeches by both Renner and Kunschak regarding the importance of continuing the coalition, on 10 June 1920 the arrangement split apart in "full public view" during a parliamentary debate.[40]

The immediate cause of the coalition breakdown was an ordinance issued from the Ministry for Military Affairs on 25 May concerning procedures governing the election of trustees in the Federal Army. The ordinance did not change or modify any provisions of the March Army Law, but clarified procedures for selection of trustees. Each company, or equivalent unit with fewer than one hundred men, was to have two trustees and two understudies. Each unit with more than a hundred men would have three. From this pool of trustees, delegates were to be chosen for the staffs of higher units. Six brigade delegates were to be attached to the Ministry for Military Affairs. Elections were to be called and arranged by existing members of the *Volkswehr* soldiers' councils who were enlisted into the Federal Army. Their role in the elections offended conservatives; Cuninghame agreed that details of the ordinance were to some extent "arbitrary and not compelled by the Army Bill."[41]

The German Nationalists, supported by many Christian Socials, introduced an interpellation in the National Assembly on 10 June in reference to Deutsch's ordinance. The bourgeois parties argued that both the Army Law and the agreement between the coalition partners required that executive orders, such as the one issued on 25 May, be submitted to the cabinet for approval, which Deutsch had not done. Deutsch replied that the matter had been settled in principle, and his ordinance was merely a matter of detail. His opponents maintained that the ordinance laid down the terms of immunity the trustees were to enjoy, and therefore went well beyond the sphere of the routine. Kunschak declared the Christian Socials could not accept the ordinance as legal until the government as a whole had approved it, and demanded that the decree be withdrawn. In response, a socialist hothead named Leuthner insisted the Social Democrats would never permit the ordinance to be withdrawn, and accused the Christian Socials of reneging on their agreement concerning the Army Bill, suggesting that the conservative party had been forced into concessions in the wake of the Kapp *Putsch,* which they now renounced. Kunschak replied that such remarks implied the coalition had come to an end. Bauer and Adler were quick to dissociate themselves from Leuthner's intemperate remarks, but they felt compelled that evening to seek and obtain their party's permission to withdraw from the coalition.[42]

Reasons given by Renner and others for withdrawing included a range of problems: negotiations on the Capital Tax Bill and on constitutional reform had reached an impasse; organization of the *Heimwehr* in Salzburg and the Tyrol, with the apparent blessing and support of the Christian Social Party and its leaders, had aggravated antagonism between the parties; attacks by some Christian Social leaders and the *Reichspost* upon the government (of which the party was a partner) caused increasing resentment among socialists; Kunschak had seriously insulted Deutsch and threatened forcibly to end the coalition during the parliamentary debate on 10 June; and the combination of bourgeois parties demanding withdrawal of the army ordinance presented the Social Democrats with an impossible demand.[43] The Christian Socials, on the other hand, blamed the socialists, and Deutsch in particular, for the split. Funder calls Deutsch's army regulation a "flagrant breach of the law, committed by no less a person than a member of the cabinet itself."[44]

The cabinet resigned on 11 June 1920, but agreed to direct affairs until a new government was formed. There was some hope for a time that a new government could be formed by reshuffling the cabinet slightly, but any chance of that was ended on 14 June, when Renner gave a speech calling the Christian Socials a "party of profiteers." The conservatives responded by declaring their intention to refuse participation in any cabinet that included either Renner or Deutsch.[45] Eventually, however, agreement was reached to form a "proportional" cabinet made up of representatives of the three parties in proportion to their strength in the National Assembly. Cabinet members were responsible only to their own parties for their actions. On 3 July the cabinet was formed. Dr. Mayr, who had been in charge of a special secretariat working to prepare a constitution, was named head of the cabinet, but did not assume the title of chancellor since he represented only his party, not the whole government. Although he resigned as chancellor, Renner retained his post as foreign secretary. Deutsch remained state secretary for military affairs. The "proportional" cabinet set elections for 17 October and agreed to pass the necessary electoral law, to pass the Capital Tax Bill, and to attempt agreement on general principles only for the constitution. Details of the constitutional arrangement would be left to those returned to power in the October elections. It is interesting to note that the offending army ordinance that had been the immediate cause of the split was not mentioned in the program outlined by the transitional government. Eventually the ordinance went into effect without fanfare or controversy, suggesting that the fundamental cause of the dissolution of the coalition had been deeper than the "relatively minor matter" of the army regulation issued by Deutsch.[46]

Responsibility for the dissolution of the coalition certainly lay with both parties, and in more sober moments, spokesmen for both groups agreed that the decision was essentially a mutual one, however noisy. Cunnighame was perhaps one of the most perceptive of observers in Vienna at the time, which makes his view of the matter a valuable one. The British attaché suggested in a lengthy report sent to London that the underlying cause of the split was the return of some stability to the country, at least to the extent that conservative groups no longer believed the Social Democrats were absolutely necessary to keep radical elements under control. Continued inflation hurt those professional and intellectual classes living on fixed incomes, while governmental policy provided for increases in workers' wages. Those groups who had believed it was necessary to agree to the commanding influence of the socialists in order to avoid "armed revolution by the mob" no longer perceived the threat as urgent and were unwilling to see socialist dominance continue any longer.[47]

The Capital Tax Bill passed on 21 July, after long debate. The parties agreed on a constitution shortly before the October elections; the document exhibited all the defects of an ideological compromise. Neither of these compromises carried over to the struggle for control of military forces in the new republic. If anything, the army question became more acute in the fall of

1920 as the election campaign got under way. The most controversial issue, which had always been a source of party antagonism, was the soldiers' councils, now called trustees. Placing the
state police under municipal jurisdiction became an election issue also, championed by the Social Democrats and opposed
adamantly by the Christian Socials.[48]

Dr. Frey, whom Deutsch had put in command of the Red
Guard in 1919 in hopes of controlling radical elements, had a
falling out with Deutsch over the issue of soldiers' councils. Frey
was not accepted into the Federal Army. The soldiers' council of
Vienna under Frey continued to function and to publish *Der freie
Soldat,* raising serious questions about who really controlled the
trustees in the new Federal Army, the Ministry for Military Affairs or the more radical and unofficial soldiers' council under
Frey.

Election of trustees began in August 1920 within units that had
reached 50 percent of authorized strength. By 21 August, that
included all units in Vienna, Lower Austria, and Carinthia. Austrian officers in the new army declared "unanimously" that the
advent of trustees adversely affected discipline, a familiar refrain long applied to soldiers' councils in the *Volkswehr.* Officers'
organizations cited an example of an order given by a battalion
commander to fetch rifles from the barracks square to squad
rooms. The order was refused, allegedly owing to trustee influence, on grounds that such work was civil, not military, and if
performed should warrant extra pay. On the other hand, the
trustees themselves usually saw their system as a safeguard
against Bolshevism, and argued that trustees intended to
strengthen discipline, not weaken it.[49]

In any case, the Christian Socials were not happy about the
direction taken by the new army. They wished to have a reliable
force at their disposal to counteract socialist influence. Their
hope was to gain political power in the October elections and
then alter the whole complexion of the Federal Army, or even
"replace it with a new organization."[50] Any future plans, however, would depend upon the approval of the Inter-Allied Control Commissions. The Control Commissions were to show little
inclination to sanction deviations from the Treaty of Saint Germain.

6

The Army of Saint Germain

MEMBERS of the Inter-Allied Control Commissions, after arrival in Austria, became visible and daily reminders to the Austrians of the "Dictate of St. Germain," and frequently bore the brunt of Austrian frustrations. As the successor, at least in function, to the hated Italian Armistice Commission, the Control Commissions generated bitter and intense feelings in the Austrian press and population. That Austria paid the cost of the Control Commissions only exacerbated the problem. Despite their unpopularity, however, and in spite of a deliberate Austrian policy of obstructionism, the Allied representatives achieved a fair degree of success in shaping the new Austrian Federal Army to the specifications laid out in the Treaty of Saint Germain.

Austria's earliest concern about the Control Commissions centered on the expected cost. In December 1919 Renner had requested informally a reduction in Control Commission size, in view of Vienna's serious financial condition.[1] In late January 1920, Austrian officials learned from the Italian Armistice Commission that nearly one hundred officers and a thousand others would be included in the Allied Control Commissions.[2] Gravely worried, Austria requested officially that the commissions be reduced.[3] The Conference of Ambassadors agreed in principle, and approved only twenty officers and eighty enlisted men for the advance echelon.[4]

Deutsch in particular objected to permitting an advance echelon to begin work before the treaty came into force. He argued in early March that Austria needed more time to get her house in order. He hoped to see passage of the Army Law before the Control Commissions arrived, and he feared—based on the German experience—that the Control Commissions would cause considerable economic disruption in Austria. Renner overruled Deutsch. Renner maintained that Austrian refusal to cooperate would create an unfavorable impression in Paris.[5] Nonetheless, Deutsch declared his intention to cause as much difficulty as he could for the Control Commissions. He assured Renner that "no stone will be left unturned" in attempting to delay the arrival of the advance echelon; after its arrival, Deutsch confidently (and accurately) predicted the Austrians could "easily impose a certain influence on the method and tempo" of Allied activity.[6] The Austrian policy of obstruction and delay was formulated before the Control Commissions set foot on Austrian soil.

Early Austrian resentment toward Allied control spread and intensified in May and June 1920, culminating in a vitriolic press campaign. The Control Commission members met for the first time on 5 May, when they discussed *inter alia* the transfer and sale by Austria of arms and ammunition to private companies and foreign nations. Local Viennese newspapers bitterly criticized the resulting Allied seizure of war matériel and a prohibition against Austrian disposal of equipment through sales.[7] The press campaign intensified after the Allies announced their intentions to prevent alienation or transformation of war matériel even though the Treaty of Saint Germain was not yet in force.

The members of the Control Commissions believed the Austrian government had condoned and encouraged the press attacks. The generals complained to Paris that the press campaign was "certainly inspired by the Government, which is seeking to gain the support of public opinion in its attitude towards the Entente."[8] The press campaign prompted the Conference of Ambassadors to warn Austria of "disagreeable consequences" that could arise from inflammatory newspaper stories.[9] The Austrian government denied responsibility for the press attacks, but acknowledged Allied concern and promised to do what it could to prevent further outbursts.[10] Ratification of the peace treaty by France in July undercut the Austrian argument that the Control Commissions had no authority to interfere in Austrian activities, and the press attacks diminished. Critical articles continued to appear from time to time, however, and in November the papers mounted a fresh attack; the casus belli stemmed from the Control Commissions' announced intention to continue working beyond the originally expected three months' duration. The Austrian press argued that matériel seized by the Allies was raw material desperately needed for Austrian industry, that Allied inventory-taking prolonged unnecessarily the Control Commission activity, and that Allied officers lived in unduly expensive style at Austrian expense.[11]

Communications between the Control Commissions and the Austrian government were usually awkward and difficult, especially before July 1920 when the Control Commissions had no official status.[12] Official communication then came directly from the Conference of Ambassadors in Paris, or, in some instances, passed through the Italian Armistice Commission in Vienna. After the treaty came into force, difficulties remained. Austrian ministries passed responsibility from one to another, until the Allies adopted the practice of sending all correspondence to the Chancellor.[13] Deutsch complained in late August that Control Commission members were interfering in the internal politics of Austria by dealing directly with provincial governors and local army commanders. On 3 September the president of the Military Control Commission responded. He informed Deutsch that the Allies had no obligation to make all contacts through the central government in Vienna and had no obligation to distinguish between Austrian internal and external policy.[14]

Communication problems were compounded by tension among the Allies. In April an Italian proposal to the Conference of Ambassadors called for Control Commission reports to go to the Italian General Staff and then to the Allied Military Committee at Versailles. The British delegate, Lord Derby, objected to the unnecessary intermediary, and succeeded in having the proposal tabled.[15] Eventually the conference reached a compromise. Communications between Paris and Vienna would be direct, but copies of reports and instructions were to be forwarded to the Italian general staff.[16] Temperley charged that Italian preoccupation with collecting the full amount of war matériel due under the Armistice of 3 November was part of the reason the Control Commissions failed to complete their work as hoped.[17]

The Military Control Commission, responsible for army affairs and army war matériel, carried the major work load of all the Control Commissions. Its presiding officer, an Italian general, was the senior Allied officer in Austria. General Luigi Zuccari could look back upon an illustrious career in the Italian army, but, unfortunately, in 1920 his best years were behind him. Austrian officers in close contact with the Control Commissions described Zuccari as an old man who liked to give the appearance of great energy, but who squandered his attention on small details. The problem was compounded by Zuccari's unwillingness to delegate responsibility. Personally likeable and even charming, Zuccari led a secluded and frugal life in Vienna's Hotel Imperial. His understanding of the Austrian situation, enhanced by good command of German and service in Berlin as an attaché before the war, and his generally sympathetic attitude toward the Austrians, were hindered by feebleness, occasional obstinacy, and his penchant for detail.[18]

French General Hallier, who served as head of the subcommission on Personnel and Army Organization, emerged after Zuccari as the second most visible Allied general in Vienna. Unlike Zuccari, Hallier pursued his tasks with great energy and resolve. Austrian intelligence on Hallier was less cordial than reports on Zuccari; Austrian liaison officers reported that Hallier's claim to be a friend of Austria was not true. His insistence on literal application of the treaty, according to the Austrians, betrayed him as an exponent of France's "Victory Policy" *(Siegespolitik)*. Hating all Germans, Hallier, the Austrians said, often revealed that "haughty arrogance so characteristic of French officers."[19] His energy and his close association with Marshal Foch soon propelled Hallier to a position of preponderance on the Military Control Commission.

Immediately upon his arrival in Vienna with the advance echelon of the Control Commissions, General Hallier established himself as an energetic champion of Saint Germain. His subcommission on Personnel and Army Organization addressed a wide range of issues that frequently involved controversial interpretation of the treaty. Hallier proved willing to take strong positions, especially concerning five main issues: the problem of Austrian army reserves, the disproportionate rank structure of the Federal Army, the question of army schools, the problem of discipline within the army, and the prospect of allowing Austria excess police and gendarmes in exchange for a reduction in the size of the Federal Army. The last two issues provide good examples of Allied arguments based on the "spirit of the treaty."

Hallier took up the question of Austrian reserves immediately in April 1920, when he challenged the Army Law of 18 March 1920, which prescribed a reserve force for the Federal Army. The Army Law obligated enlisted men to serve at least twelve years, six on active duty and six in the reserves. Reserve service required men to respond to a recall order for active service, although reserves were to be mobilized only in case of extraordinary events.[20] On 5 May the Military Control Commission sent a note to the Austrian government over Zuccari's signature, declaring the Army Law contrary to Saint Germain; the offending clauses in the law were numbers 5, 12, 15, 16, 18, 20 and 23. Pointing out that Article 120 of the peace treaty permitted 30,000 troops but prohibited reserves, Zuccari asked to be informed how Austria intended to alter the Army Law.[21]

In their reply, the Austrians explained that reserves called for in the Army Law did not have the character of military forces prohibited by the treaty. The reserves envisioned in the Army Law merely provided replacements should that army fall below 30,000.[22]

Discrepancies in the Treaty of Saint Germain easily led to differing interpretations concerning army reserves. Article 122 clearly forbade reserves in any normal sense of the term, holding that "all measures of mobilization, or appertaining to mobilization" were forbidden. Article 126, on the other hand, stipulated that the twelve-year period of enlistment for soldiers in the army should include "at least 6 years with the colors." One could easily infer that six of the twelve years might be served in some sort of reserve status.

The Conference of Ambassadors considered the reserve issue in early June 1920, and ruled in favor of the Allied Military Committee at Versailles, which unanimously rejected the Austrian interpretation. Foch's committee declared the 30,000 figure included "reserves," who, if not on active duty, must be considered on indefinite leave. These nonactive duty soldiers had to be carried on rosters, and could not be replaced until the expiration of their twelfth year.[23] Austria thereupon requested clarification of Article 126, which required six years "with the colors."[24] In response, the Allies explained that reserves as such were clearly forbidden by Article 122. Article 126, however, had been written to permit Austria to maintain fewer than 30,000 men on active duty if the Austrians chose not to maintain full ranks for twelve years.[25] Eichoff's further attempts in Paris to persuade the conference to reconsider were rebuffed. Austria, the conference explained, should deal directly with the Control Commissions in Vienna. Eichoff remarked bitterly to his government that the Military Control Commission had obviously taken great pains to argue its position to the Paris Conference of Ambassadors, and had conducted a "flanking movement" to do so.[26]

Eichoff's frustration was that of a man whose own flanking movement had failed.

In October, two months later, Austria received a small concession concerning the twelve-year commitment. The government had appealed to Paris for relief, citing inconveniences entailed by enlisting an army of 30,000 en masse with all recruits expected to complete their obligation at the same time in 1932. Austria asked that certain provisions of the Army Law be allowed to stand: former Habsburg or *Volkswehr* soldiers should be able to contract for shorter terms of enlistment by allowing earlier service to count toward twelve years; new soldiers could be enlisted at the rate of 3,100 per year to replace those Habsburg and *Volkswehr* men who reached the end of their contracts. Upon the recommendation of the Military Control Commission, the Conference of Ambassadors approved the Austrian request on 20 October.[27]

The Military Control Commission enjoyed greater success in obtaining support from the Conference of Ambassadors than it did in persuading Austria to change her laws as required. In early November, Zuccari reminded the Austrians that the Army Law and certain regulations must be changed.[20] Hallier reiterated the demand, "inviting" the Austrians to annul all laws passed before 4 November 1918 that pertained to recruiting and organization of the old Habsburg army and those related to measures of mobilization.[29] In mid-December, the Conference of Ambassadors threatened vague economic sanctions if Austria failed to revise military legislation and abrogate mobilization laws.[30] Hallier demanded again in January 1921 that changes be made in the Army Law. He told the new Austrian minister of interior, Egon Glanz, that revisions must be completed by February when the Control Commissions were scheduled to terminate.[31] Legislation containing modifications demanded by the Allies was finally introduced in the Austrian National Council on 3 February, only to be met by violent protest from noncommissioned officers of the old Habsburg army. They feared the professional noncommissioned officer would become an endangered species, suffering discharge and replacement by regular officers of the old army.[32] Delays continued into March, when the Allied Liquidation Organ—successor to the Inter-Allied Control Commissions—under the direction of Hallier, insisted that necessary laws be amended by 15 April 1921.[33] The diplomatic language became less friendly as Hallier expressed disbelief that the Austrian government could not find time to pass the required legislation.[34] The 15 April deadline arrived, only to have the Austrians report that a subcommittee had been formed under the legislative Army Committee to iron out the required changes.[35] Not until 28 April 1921 was a bill passed that modified the Army Law of March 1920.[36]

Hallier experienced even greater frustration and exasperation when he attempted to reduce the Federal Army's high proportion of senior officers. He had long been concerned about the large number of field grade officers and the small number of company grade officers, especially lieutenants. In March 1921 he requested more information on an Austrian scheme designed to reduce the top-heavy grade structure.[37] In July, Hallier found an unlikely ally in the socialist *Arbeiter Zeitung,* which criticized the Christian Social minister for army affairs, Carl Vaugoin, for the disproportionately high number of field grade officers in the Army.[38] In August, the Liquidation Organ demanded figures comparing the rank structure before the March 1920 Army Law with the hierarchy in the summer of 1921.[39] Austria reported that 1,025 of 1,500 officers held the higher ranks, compared to 625–650 field grade officers before the Army Law.[40] Hallier expressed his concern about the matter to Foch in a letter urging that the Conference of Ambassadors approach Austria about the problem. Foch responded by inviting Hallier to present proposals to fix the proper proportion of field grade officers in the Federal Army.[41] As a result, Hallier told the Austrians to estimate the time it would take to reduce the imbalance so that he could make proper recommendations to Paris.[42]

The Austrians were naturally indignant that Hallier had presumed to address himself to any imbalance in the Federal Army's rank structure. They replied that the treaty did not specify the number of "staff officers." In any case, the ministry for military affairs would need time to correct a situation that was the result of unusual circumstances.[43] Undaunted, Hallier notified the Austrians in October that Foch's committee had decided Austria must reduce the number of staff officers to 650. Hallier demanded that plans for the necessary reduction be forwarded to the Liquidation Organ by 15 November.[44] The Austrian ministry for military affairs urged the Austrian government to refuse cooperation. On 9 November, the ministry for military affairs recommended taking a stand based on the illegality of Hallier's demand. The treaty simply limited the officer corps to

1,500—no rank structure was prescribed. Noting that the Liquidation Organ had cited the "spirit of St. Germain," the ministry urged that Austria take a firm stand.[45] The ministry admitted that the Entente could, of course, work its will if it wanted to badly enough. Hallier demonstrated his willingness to do so in December, when he warned that if he did not have a satisfactory answer by 7 December, the Liquidation Organ would formulate its own plan for reorganizing the Federal Army.[46] The Austrians responded with a clever and complicated scheme that avoided the pensioning off of "excess" staff officers by simply changing duty-titles.[47] Austria succeeded in frustrating Hallier's intentions. A year later the Liquidation Organ was still trying unsuccessfully to persuade Austria to reduce the number of "superior" officers in the Federal Army.[48]

Hallier's greatest concern, shared by Allied representatives in Paris, had focused early on discipline in the Federal Army. The French general disliked the notion of a "democratic" army, and rarely missed an opportunity to denounce the influence of soldiers' councils in the Federal Army.[49] The soldiers' councils harbored a reciprocal dislike for the Control Commissions. In August 1920, Allied representatives, acting on secretly received information, located 30,000 unauthorized rifles in Viennese barracks, and 4,000 in Wiener Neustadt.[50] Spokesmen for the soldiers' councils charged that Austrian officers, sympathetic to the Entente and its Control Commissions, had covertly led the Allies to the discovery. Dr. Frey and his clique (called the "Working Community of Revolutionary Socialists") cited the discovery of hidden arms in the barracks as an excuse for arming the proletariat against the cabal of Austrian conservatives and the capitalist Entente.[51]

In 1920 Frey no longer enjoyed the official status that had been his in the *Volkswehr*.[52] Frey was sympathetic to the Communists, although he refused to join the party. He considered himself a leftist Social Democrat, albeit one who was out of step with the socialist party leadership. Differences of opinion and approach between Frey and Deutsch on the issue of soldiers' councils led to a falling out between the two men. Frey was excluded from the new Federal Army. Frey advocated a dominant role for soldiers' councils and retained his unofficial leadership of the soldiers' council organization. The soldiers' councils hierarchy from the *Volkswehr* days enjoyed no governmental sanction, but Frey's group included many of the same people who had joined the new Federal Army and served therein as trustees. Frey's influence and his potential for disrupting things, therefore, was considerable. On 16 September, a meeting of the Social Democratic Party dealt with Frey and his unwillingness to cooperate with the party leadership. A vote of those present overwhelmingly opposed Frey and accused him of breach of discipline. The vote declared support for party solidarity at Frey's expense.[53] As a result, Frey formed his own party in December 1920. The "Socialist Labor Party of German-Austria (Left)" staked out a position between the Social Democrats and the Communists; Frey called for joining the Third International and opening negotiations with the Communist Party in Austria.[54]

In mid-October 1920, the Conference of Ambassadors considered the question of Austrian soldiers' councils, or trustees. (Opponents rarely distinguished between the two.) The conference concluded the issue was outside its jurisdiction, but agreed with Hallier that something should be done. The Allies believed the soldiers' councils to be incompatible with a Federal Army charged with maintaining order, its mission prescribed by Article 120 of the Treaty of Saint Germain. The Conference of Ambassadors stopped short of seeking complete suppression of the trustee system, but believed some changes in the Austrian Army Law were necessary to make the system compatible with discipline. Conference members agreed that each representative would have his own government express concern to Austria, since the conference should not officially address an issue outside its jurisdiction.[55]

The conference also decided to have Cambon, as president of the group, call upon Eichoff to discuss unofficially the Allied concern about discipline in the Federal Army. In the meantime, Zuccari transmitted the conference position to the Austrian government.[56] When Cambon discussed the matter with Eichoff, the Austrian agreed completely that discipline in the Federal Army was deplorable. Choosing this moment to raise again the whole question of a professional army instead of a militia, Eichoff expressed greater concern about discipline than Cambon.[57] Eichoff claimed the Austrian government was helpless to control the ruffians who made up the army, which was composed of the "worst elements" from the *Volkswehr*. The only hope, Eichoff proclaimed, was a revision of Saint Germain to allow a militia composed of peasants, "very fine fellows who would make a well-disciplined army."[58] The Conference of Ambassadors, to no one's surprise, soundly rejected Eichoff's suggestion that the treaty be revised.

Eventually the solution to the problem of discipline emerged from Austrian domestic politics rather than from Entente policy. Schober told Lindley in November 1920 that Allied agitation for an improvement in army discipline would amount to nothing. Schober said the solution would come from his own intention to create a reliable force over the next several months.[59] The Social Democrats quickly lined up in opposition to Schober's efforts to curb the influence of socialist trustees; Bauer announced in a speech on 5 November that the socialist party would definitely fill the role of an opposition party until public opinion in Austria recalled the party to rule when it would create a true socialist program. Bauer claimed the most important role for the party was defense of the new army and protection from reactionary attacks on it. There was little doubt that socialists played a dominant role in the new army, even though the party had been removed from office. Lindley remarked that establishment of a "Social Democratic guard under the guise of a national army" was the most enduring achievement of the socialist party during the period of coalition.[60]

Charging repeatedly that the Federal Army was an exclusively socialist preserve, conservatives in Austria demanded an army that represented their interests, an army that would protect peasants and shopkeepers as well as the proletariat.[61] The popularity of *Heimwehr* organizations in the early 1920s reflected the association of the legal Federal Army with proletarian interests. The socialist complexion of the army, however, changed step-by-step under the guidance of Carl Vaugoin. This Christian Social minister for military affairs worked cautiously and carefully to establish army discipline and eliminate socialist dominance. Vaugoin's strategy included encouragement of a proliferation of military unions and associations representing socialist sentiments. He was careful not to attack the trustee system as such, but rather encouraged nonsocialists to fill the positions.

Having assumed the position of minister for military affairs in the reshuffled cabinet in April 1921, Vaugoin immediately set the tone for his campaign. Instructions issued from his office warned that trustees should not be criticized or taken to task for actions that were justified by their duties as trustees.[62] At the same time, Vaugoin discharged a number of soldiers from the Federal Army whose conduct and character suggested they were trouble-makers. Vaugoin's campaign was not an immediate success, but in the long run he succeeded in his goal. Before that happened, however, he suffered a number of setbacks. In June 1921 he temporarily lost his position as minister in another cabinet reorganization. Schober formed a cabinet based upon an agreement between the Christian Socials and the German Nationalists that each party would have only one deputy in the cabinet. The Christian Socials chose one of their own—Dr. Gürtler—for finance minister. Vaugoin stepped down, replaced by Colonel Joseph Wächter, a nonparty official.[63]

Elections in the Federal Army for trustees in September 1921 produced an overwhelming Social Democratic victory, because conservatives refrained from voting.[64] In November, German Nationalist deputies introduced an interpellation in the National Council that accused trustees of interfering with officers' command and authority. The German Nationalist deputies demanded that "Soldiers' Council" activity be strictly curtailed according to law, that offenders be punished, and the whole trustee system be modified.[65] Little could be done at the time, but Vaugoin eventually achieved all of these demands by following his policy of gradually eliminating socialist power and influence.

The issue of discipline was one of the few that Austrians were permitted to solve by themselves. The Austrians were hardly masters in their own house while Allied control mechanisms operated in Vienna. The issue of army schools demonstrated vividly that Austria had no choice but to dance to the Entente tune. In October 1920 the Military Control Commission studied an Austrian plan for eight different army schools. The complicated Austrian scheme led the Control Commission to refer the question to Paris, since the treaty seemed to prohibit schools other than those designed to train candidates for officer positions.[66]

Article 127: The number of students admitted to attend the courses in military schools shall be strictly in proportion to the vacancies to be filled in the cadres of officers. The students and the cadres shall be included in the effectives fixed by Article 120.

Consequently all military schools not required for this purpose shall be abolished.

The Austrian school plan called for additional schools that would provide midcareer training for officers. The Allied Military Committee of Versailles recommended to the Conference of

Ambassadors that Austria be limited to schools for commissioning officers. The conference agreed, noting that the Federal Army's mission consisted only of a police role, which required no higher professional training for officers once commissioned.[67] Zuccari informed the Austrians in late December 1920 that only schools designed to train recruits for a commission were authorized.[68]

In January 1921 Austria appealed to Hallier that the Allies reconsider their ruling on army schools. In February the ministry for foreign affairs instructed Eichoff to seek reversal of the Allied position in Paris.[69] At the same time, Austria proceeded to establish a special school in Vienna and Enns that provided six-month-long preparatory courses for *Volkswehr* lieutenants who sought commissions in the Federal Army. The Austrian government decided to pursue the question of schools against the dictates of the Entente, and have the issue brought eventually to a court of arbitration.[70] In the meantime, the Austrians intended to delay as long as possible in Vienna.[71]

The delay did not work. Hallier's demand for an answer intensified, until he let it be known in early April he was "urgently, impatiently awaiting" a reply on the question of schools.[72] Simultaneously, the Conference of Ambassadors rejected the Austrian appeal for reconsideration of the issue.[73] Yielding to Hallier's demands, the ministry for foreign affairs agreed to have the ministry for military affairs prepare a plan for a new scheme for army schools. Despite the prospect of an arbitration hearing, the Austrian government agreed to submit—at least temporarily—in hopes of satisfying the Entente and bringing the Liquidation Organ to an early end.[74] The ministry for military affairs reluctantly submitted a plan, warning that it could become a permanent fixture if the anticipated hearing in court were to result in a ruling favorable to the Entente.[75] The new plan for schools, submitted to the Liquidation Organ on 20 April, gained Allied approval. Hallier requested that applicable laws and regulations be changed by 5 May to reflect the new army school system.[76]

In June the ministry for military affairs finally issued an order modifying the army's school system. All regulations and statutes pertaining to the so-called School for Army Leaders and Instructors were canceled. The new school, divided into courses for officer aspirants, courses in physical training, and training courses for riding and driving, was named simply the Army School. A proposed Army Troop School was not to be established, but special courses for *Volkswehr* lieutenants in Vienna and Enns were to continue for a limited time.[77] The Liquidation Organ approved guidelines setting up the Army School, but disapproved an order published in July concerning training for noncommissioned officers.[78] The order established a one-year school to commence 1 October 1921, which would train selected private soldiers for promotion to noncommissioned officer rank. The Liquidation Organ considered the details contrary to Saint Germain, because the school provided instruction for more soldiers than there were vacancies in the ranks. The ministry for military affairs annulled the order on 28 July in accordance with Allied demands.[79]

Hallier did not limit his attention to the Federal Army proper. He played an important role in the difficult issue of reducing Austrian police and gendarmerie to the limits required by Saint Germain. Domestic Austrian politics complicated the problem, which centered on allowing Austria to keep the excess police if compensatory reductions were made in the size of the Federal Army.

In the spring of 1920, before the ruling coalition in Austria had broken apart, agreement on the police issue appeared to be within easy reach. The Allied powers favored the arrangement, conservatives enthusiastically endorsed it, and Social Democratic leaders expressed willingness to suffer reductions in the army in order to retain current levels of strength in the police and gendarmerie. Deutsch and Colonel Körner, commander of the *Volkswehr,* supported Schober's plan to retain 7,800 city police, which exceeded limits set by Saint Germain by 2,500, and maintenance of 8,300 gendarmes, 2,300 more than permitted under the treaty.[80]

The coalition collapse in the summer and the rhetoric of election campaigning in the autumn of 1920 destroyed the spirit of cooperation and accommodation that had prevailed in the spring. As the army became ever more closely identified with the socialists, and the police and gendarmerie with the conservatives, the police-and-army issue grew more complicated. Relations among workers' councils, Social Democratic leaders, the Federal Army, Schober and his police, and Christian Social politicians had never been simple. As Cuninghame observed, the army and the police tended to serve as buffers between political antagonists: the "people" would not attack the army in the streets, nor would the army fire on the police.[81]

Socialist concern for protecting the leftist element in Schober's forces surfaced in December 1920, when some members of the city police and the city guard participated in a demonstration against high prices. Schober warned against such activity and threatened disciplinary action in the future. The Social Democrats attacked Schober viciously, claiming he had infringed upon policemen's rights as citizens. Socialist leaders attempted to soften public criticism by visiting Schober privately to explain that the public outcry had been necessary to mollify the Social Democratic rank and file.[82] Nonetheless, interparty suspicions created a climate of distrust in 1921 that hindered peaceful settlement of the police-and-army issue.

The Western Allies had always been disposed to approve police forces beyond the limits of Saint Germain, provided commensurate reductions took place in the army. In December 1920 the Conference of Ambassadors officially sanctioned the scheme, but insisted on a twelve-year enlistment for the police and gendarmerie to prevent the enlarged police forces from being transformed into a short-term army. The conference agreed wholeheartedly with Foch's committee that approval would help Austria to recruit a smaller but more reliable army.[83] The Austrians saw no problem in the twelve-year minimum enlistment inasmuch as police usually served for thirty-five years before civil service retirement.[84]

In February 1921 the Allies clarified their position. Minimum service of twelve years would permit further increases in the police and gendarmerie as long as the total number of extra police and army effectives remained below 30,000.[85] However, the apparently smooth progress toward resolution of the police and army issue was stymied by Hallier's objections. The French general insisted that Austria pass legislation or issue formal regulations that would commit Austria to the understanding. Schober fully intended to limit the combination of police and army effectives to levels agreeable to the Allies, but volatile Social Democratic opposition to deeper cuts in the Federal Army made any formal agreement difficult. The British and American representatives in Vienna urged the Conference of Ambassadors to let the matter rest temporarily. Lindley observed that even in February 1921 the army was still a "notorious Social Democratic party" instrument that the government hoped eventually to reduce, but without attracting attention. The British diplomat urged a "broad interpretation" of Saint Germain, which would permit excess police without formal Austrian agreement to a reduction in the army. The British and American argument stressed that recruiting for the Federal Army had fallen far short of 30,000, so Austria—for the moment at least—had a combined police, gendarmerie, and army well under the total permissible number. The French, however, despite firm philosophical support for Schober's position, opposed a "broad interpretation" of Saint Germain, without formal agreement, out of fear the Germans would use the precedent to alter the Treaty of Versailles.[86] In May 1921, therefore, the Military Control Commission demanded that Schober reduce the police and gendarmerie to the size stipulated by the peace treaty. Schober complained to the Allies that the demand left him only two choices: enlist the surplus police into the Federal Army or discharge the surplus. The Social Democrats violently opposed the first solution, and Schober told the American representative in Vienna he would resign if forced to discharge the surplus police, because he could no longer guarantee law and order.[87]

None of the Allies wanted Schober to resign. To them he was a major contributor to Austrian stability. A change in the French position, or at least divergence between French diplomats and French military men, broke the impasse. On 19 May the French minister in Vienna joined his British and American colleagues in urging his government to adopt a broad interpretation of Saint Germain that would tacitly treat the extra police and gendarmerie as part of the Federal Army.[88] Italy agreed. Italy generally favored the Social Democrats, but feared that serious disruption of Austrian peace and order might turn against Italian interests. The Liquidation Organ's attitude softened considerably following the French representative's recommendation to Paris, but Hallier still presented a position in Vienna somewhat harsher than the attitude taken by the Conference of Ambassadors. The general continued to expect the Austrian government to consider officially the issue of surplus police forces and corresponding army reductions.[89] The Conference of Ambassadors, on the other hand, was content to hear that Austria "intended" to reduce gradually the excess police and would agree to provide "facilities" that would allow the Liquidation Organ to verify the combined number of police, gendarmerie, and army effectives.[90] By the end of 1921, Hallier had fallen into step with the prevailing attitude in Paris. In late December, he was content merely to admonish Austria to suspend army recruiting until normal attrition from the police and gendarmerie reduced force levels to agreed-upon limits.[91]

Austria's choice to maintain an overage of police and a reduced number of army effectives was dictated by the government's dismal failure to attract a full complement of army recruits. By August 1920 only Carinthia had reached its quota; for all of Austria, only 20,791 private soldiers had applied for 26,500 posts.[92] Six months later, Vaugoin reported that fewer than 20,000 private soldiers were in the army—nearly 6,500 under the quota.[93] The Social Democrats accused conservative governmental officials of deliberately reducing the army as part of a conspiracy against the socialists, but Baron Glanz explained that between 10 percent and 15 percent of those accepted for duty in the army opted instead for higher-paying civilian employment. Furthermore, a prohibition against cross-provincial recruiting impeded progress toward recruiting the full authorization.[94]

In February 1921 new legislation provided pay increase, additional family allowances, and provision for a substantial bonus upon completion of service, but recruiting results failed to improve. Moreover, on 1 July 1921, a number of soldiers were discharged for concealing character defects that disqualified them for service. According to Vaugoin, enlisted strength dropped to 19,000, only 72 percent of the quota.[95]

The Burgenland crisis improved—at least temporarily—both recruiting efforts and discipline within the Federal Army. The peace treaty with Hungary signed at Trianon in June 1920 awarded the Burgenland to Austria. In August 1921, Austria attempted unsuccessfully to take possession of the province. Advancing columns of Austrian gendarmerie were turned back by insurgent Hungarian bands supported covertly by the government in Budapest. The Austrian failure to occupy the Burgenland with gendarmes forced the government to turn to the suspect Federal Army.

In an effort to bring the army up to strength, the ministry for military affairs conducted a vigorous recruiting drive in the autumn of 1921. A favorable socialist press campaign helped Vienna and Lower Austria to approach their full quotas. The patriotic appeal against Horthy's Hungarians, however, made slight impression in the rural Austrian provinces. The government resorted to easing restrictions on recruiting (such as age requirements) and temporarily suspended voluntary retirements.[96] As a result, by the end of 1921 the total army strength had risen to slightly more than 25,000.[97]

Military occupation of the Burgenland, begun 13 November

1921, was completed by 4 December. The field activity worked a salutary effect on discipline and morale. The action reduced friction between commissioned and noncommissioned ranks, and reduced the influence and activity of trustees.[98] By all accounts, the Federal Army surprised its many critics with a demonstration of good discipline and effective combat action.[99] The army, which emerged from its first real test under fire, pleased almost everyone. The Social Democrats considered the Federal Army their own, and were justly proud of its success in the Burgenland. The conservatives sensed a movement within the army toward a nonsocialist orientation and optimistically looked to the future. The Allies were content that Saint Germain had created an army that posed no threat to Austria's neighbors, but one which served well to safeguard Austrian interests.

7

The Spoils of War

DESPITE success in shaping the Federal Army to their liking, the Western powers were only partly successful in imposing the Treaty of Saint Germain. Problems had plagued disarmament efforts from the moment the Control Commissions had begun to organize. Locating and collecting war matériel, munitions, and arms proved to be particularly difficult; failure to accomplish these tasks as planned forced the Allies to extend their stay in Austria well beyond original expectations.

The delay of nearly a year between treaty-signing and the onset of Allied control in Austria made location of war matériel much more complicated than it would have been had the Control Commissions begun their work immediately. The dispersion of matériel to foreign buyers, private export firms, and the general population, was coupled with the Austrian policy of obstructionism and delay that frustrated Allied attempts to strip the country of unauthorized weapons.

At its best, Allied confiscation of surplus war equipment was a first step toward world wide disarmament. At its worst, the same activity could be seen as a mad scramble for the defeated enemy's resources under pretense of reducing the world's armaments. There were three categories of spoils: aeronautical equipment and matériel; naval vessels and associated equipment; and "war material," which included army equipment, arms, ammunition, and the means to produce them.

The Naval Control Commission caused the least disturbance in Austria. The Habsburg fleet in the Adriatic and most of the vessels in the Danube flotilla fell into the possession of other states. The Austrians were quite content to stay out of the Italian-Yugloslav squabbles over the disposition of the Habsburg fleet.

Disposition of army war matériel posed considerably more difficulty. In the Military Control Commission, Italian Brigadier General Garrone served as president of the subcommission on armaments, which had responsibility for war matériel. Austrian reports sketched a man with an air of wealth and influence, yet one who showed himself to be personally likeable, charming, sensitive, and a devoted family man. At the same time, regarding his official duties, he was, in Austrian eyes, a strait-laced, nar-row-minded technocrat. Austrian observers criticized his ad-ministrative methods as clumsy and awkward. Austrians accused Garrone of presiding over a chaotic and complicated system of taking inventory.[1] Garrone, on the other hand, was quick to find fault with the Austrians. According to his own account (to the Conference of Ambassadors), his stream of notes and requests to the Austrians grew in volume and complexity because Austrian officials responded with "incomplete and inac-curate" information, and only after long delays.[2]

The problem of Austrian war matériel had surfaced in Paris as early as July 1919, even before the peace treaty had been com-pleted and signed. The newly formed Council of the Heads of Delegations was surprised to learn on 25 July that Austria was turning over arms and equipment to the Italian mission in Vienna, which in turn passed the matériel on to Czechoslovakia. The council posed four questions to the Entente military repre-sentatives in Paris: Who gave consent for this activity? Had arms gone to the Italian mission only, or to the Italians and the French jointly? How long had this been going on? How much had been transferred to the Czechs?[3]

Answers to these questions revealed that Central Europe had witnessed a series of developments in early 1919 only dimly understood by Allied representatives in Paris. In May 1919 the Czechoslovak government had sought help in the face of Hun-garian military advances. The Czechs requested, through the French representative in Vienna, cession of Austrian arms and ammunition with which to fight Béla Kun. The request was passed to General Segre, who approved wholeheartedly, but sought official sanction from the Allies in Paris. Foch replied from Paris that Czechoslovakia's army should be supplied by the Italian Armistice Commission from stocks of Austro-Hungarian war matériel.[4] The action was taken in the belief that the Council of Four had approved the transfer on 9 June. But Clemenceau, who had been present on 9 June, claimed on 25 July that he had never heard a word about it.[5] In any case, in August the council approved Segre's initiative. Information furnished to the council on 1 August implied that the matériel in question was the Czechoslovak share of Austro-Hungarian stocks, whose delivery was simply accelerated in order to fight the Hungarian Bolshevik menace. The Allied representatives apparently assumed the transfers were to be a one-time event.

In early 1920 the Allies discovered that the transfer of arms from Austria to Czechoslovakia was still going on and had blossomed into big business. In February 1920, reports in two Vienna newspapers announced that the government was about to begin manufacture of ammunition at the Blumau factory in order to meet the Czech demand, and that the factory would employ some 5,000 workers. Renner and Deutsch denied that the Blumau factory was to manufacture ammunition, but neither denied intentions to sell ammunition to Czechoslovakia.[6] The *Reichspost* responded to Deutsch's denial by claiming that factories at Blumau and Wöllersdorf employed a number of workmen greatly in excess of peacetime requirements. At Wöllersdorf, according to the Christian Social newspaper, ammunition was being made or modified for Czechoslovakia. The paper referred specifically to some 10,000 rounds of ammunition for antiaircraft guns, and noted that great amounts of ammunition destined for Prague were stored at Steinfeld.[7]

Desperate for credits, Austria had little else but arms and equipment to exchange for food and coal. In addition to Czechoslovakian sales, Austria had committed herself in February 1920 to ship nearly sixty million crowns' worth of arms and ammunition to Poland in exchange for oil and other critically needed supplies.[8] Austrian arms production was a poorly kept secret. On 19 April, apparent arson at a cartridge factory at Hirtenberg in Lower Austria caused the destruction of twenty-four of twenty-nine buildings. Police suspected Communists, since it was well known that the output of ammunition at the factory was destined for Poland, then at war with Lenin's Russia.[9] If further proof of arms production was needed, the Austrian government provided it in the summer of 1920. On 2 June a workers' council passed a resolution demanding suspension of delivery of arms to Poland and to Horthy's Hungary. An official governmental reply stated that "for months" no arms or ammunition had been delivered.[10] The reply, of course, embodied a tacit admission that arms delivery had taken place in the recent past.

Austrian arms sales concerned the Conference of Ambassadors. In March 1920 the Italian military mission in Vienna—not involved in arms transfers to third powers since the summer before—complained to Paris that Austria was selling huge quantities of war matériel to private firms, which then exported the matériel to eager foreign buyers in Central Europe. An Italian protest to the Austrian government had achieved nothing.[11] Therefore, even though treaty ratification was still pending, the Conference of Ambassadors took steps to stop the alienation of war matériel, which the Allies intended to control as their own. On 1 April the conference agreed that the individual Allied governments should request Vienna to stop transfer of arms and equipment to third parties, whether private firms or foreign buyers.[12]

Renner reacted cleverly to admonitions by the British and Italian governments. He blamed the French. He readily admitted Poland and Czechoslovakia had been sold Austrian arms, but, he asserted, at French request. British and Italian suspicions were only enhanced by the fact that the French had not joined them, as of 26 April, in making appeals to Vienna on the matter of arms sales. The issue was aired in a conference meeting on 4 May. The French purported to be as mystified as the other Allies, and promised to investigate the matter.[13]

Two weeks later, Cambon reported that a French investigation of the question showed Renner to be responsible for the misunderstanding among the Allies. Renner's contention that the French had requested the transfer of arms to Czechoslovakia apparently referred to the summer of 1919, when the Allies had approved arms transfers to Prague via the Italian Armistice Commission. Renner had done nothing to dispel the ambiguity that led the British and the Italians to suspect French duplicity. When confronted directly by French investigators, Renner admitted that the French mission in Vienna had never undertaken any negotiations suggesting approval of war matériel sales.[14]

The Austrian case, however, did not rest solely on the false allegation that France had requested the sales. Austria insisted upon her right to dispose of the matériel until the treaty came into force—which required ratification by at least three of the principal Allied and associated Powers. In response to an Allied note demanding control of war depots, Deutsch replied that he believed Austria could dispose of war matériel any way she chose until the treaty came into force. An Austrian note to the Conference of Ambassadors dated 14 May 1920 protested Allied demands that Austria suspend sales of war matériel. The Austrians argued that the treaty did not forbid such activity before ratification, and prohibition of sales would hurt Austria economically.[15]

Ultimately, Austria's best argument proved to be the economic one. In a meeting of the Conference of Ambassadors on 5 June, four Austrian arguments were discussed. Austria maintained that the Allies had no legal authority to control war matériel until at least three powers had ratified the treaty. Furthermore, the powers in the past had approved Austria's attempts to secure food credits by selling war matériel. Third, war matériel provided Austrian industry an important source of raw material. And finally, Austria believed the Inter-Allied Control Commissions were supposed to facilitate economic recovery, not hinder it. Without abrogating their right to control the war matériel, the Allies sought ways to accommodate Austrian economic needs. Mr. Wallace, American representative to the Conference of Ambassadors, suggested that the conference would contradict its own policy of seeking Austrian economic recovery if it were to insist upon complete control of war matériel. Italy's Count Longare agreed only in part, for Italy objected to Austrian sales of military hardware and supplies to neighboring countries in Central Europe. Lord Derby agreed that selling matériel to neighboring countries violated the principles "which guided the Peace Conference." The conference finally agreed to instruct the Control Commissions to discriminate between war matériel "properly so-called" and matériel adaptable for civilian purposes. Furthermore, the Military Control Commission was directed to contact the Austrian section of the Reparations Commission in order to effect sales of war matériel adaptable for civilian use, which would allow Austria to obtain credits necessary for food and economic recovery.[16] In late June, the Conference of Ambassadors complicated even further the work of the Control Commissions. The conference ruled that surplus war matériel, which by treaty must be handed over for Control Commission destruction, could be sold without being destroyed if adaptable to "civil purposes."[17]

The Allied accommodation to Austria's economic needs included only war matériel adaptable for civil use, or military equipment transformed into industrial raw material after it had been rendered useless for purposes of war. The Conference of Ambassadors hoped to reduce the quantity of arms in all of Central Europe, an ambition demonstrated by a decision taken on 8 October 1920. The conference decided that war matériel of Russian origin be destroyed or rendered unserviceable under supervision of the Inter-Allied Control Commissions. Proceeds from sales of the debris by the Reparations Commission were to go to "states formed out of former Russia."[18]

The Allies continued to insist that Austria had no right to sell war matériel outright to other countries. After French ratification of Saint Germain on 16 July 1920, the controversy centered on sales that had taken place before that date. The Austrians maintained that before 16 July 1920 they had the right to transform matériel for peaceful purposes or to sell it as military equipment to interested buyers. The Conference of Ambassadors, although unanimous in opposition to the Austrian position, decided in October 1920 to refer the question to a panel of jurists.[19] In late November, upon legal advice and the precedent of the Treaty of Versailles, the conference concluded that Austria's obligation to deliver war matériel in accordance with the peace treaty began 7 November 1919, when Austria ratified the treaty. Actual transfer of ownership of the matériel to the powers was effective on 16 July 1920.[20] The decision of the conference in effect denied Austria's right to dispose of matériel after 7 November 1919, but also denied the Control Commissions' right to take control of the equipment in question before July 1920. The practical effect, of course, was to vindicate the position of the Control Commissions.

Allied hopes for universal disarmament led to prohibition against delivery of matériel that had been purchased after 7 November 1919 to the so-called Little Entente. The high principles of arms limitation were not applied so rigorously, however, when they applied to the Western powers themselves. Lord Derby wanted all the Allies to destroy the war matériel turned over to them in Austria, but his argument failed to carry the day. Italy in particular insisted that each power have latitude to dispose of its share of Austrian war matériel in any way it saw fit. The Conference of Ambassadors eventually agreed to allow each power to decide what to do with the matériel it received from Austria.[21] Matériel not suitable for fighting purposes would be disposed of by the Reparations Commission.[22] War matériel that had military value was divided among the Allies as follows: France, 11 percent; Great Britain, 8 percent; the United States, 4 percent; Serbia, 4 percent; Japan, 3 percent; and Italy, 70 percent. Italy agreed on 9 December 1920 that no further searches would be conducted for "armistice material."[23]

Despite Allied prohibition against arms sales, the illegal traffic continued. Control of contraband proved to be practically impossible, especially across Austria's border with Bavaria and along the Danube, which provided easy and quick transportation out of Austria. Allied concern for the problem was expressed in a conference meeting in early December 1920, when all agreed the Austrian government must pay for a barge load of war matériel shipped to Hungary in July.[24] Allied efforts to relieve Austria's deplorable economic condition complicated the enforcement of the ban on export of war matériel. The Conference of Ambassadors agreed that Austria could sell for export matériel that had no combat uses.[25] The difficulty, of course, was determining which matériel could be used for "fighting purposes" and which matériel could be approved for export in order to "facilitate the resumption of economic life in Austria."[26] The conference approved a list of specific articles that were to be prohibited, including guns, howitzers, gun mounts, ammunition, mortars, sabres, aiming devices, grenades, armored vehicles, protected trains, and field-radio equipment. The list was subject to revision, but at least allowed Austria to maintain such important industries as the leather industry, which produced harnesses, belts, straps, and other equipment technically falling into the category of "war material."[27]

In late December the Military Control Commission reported to the Conference of Ambassadors that a considerable amount of contraband war matériel from Germany and Austria, shipped on the Danube, was evading control by the Allies. The Danube International Navigation Commission, set up by the Allies, had no control over contraband, and in fact, was charged with facilitating trade on the river. Concerned about complete lack of control after dissolution of the Control Commissions, the Conference of Ambassadors agreed to form a Commission of Supervision, which would attempt to control illegal arms traffic on the Danube after the Control Commissions were disbanded.[28]

Manufacture of small arms in Austria presented problems in the overall attempts to disarm the area. Owing to problems of unemployment and the need for industrial enterprise throughout the country, Austria requested in late December 1920 that several factories be allowed to manufacture arms for the Federal Army. The Allies rejected the request, as Article 122 clearly specified a single governmental factory.[29] The difficulties in enforcing disarmament were again illustrated in February 1921, when the question of sporting arms came up in Paris. The Military Committee of Versailles wanted to prohibit Austrian manufacture of sporting firearms with a calibre smaller than that used by the Federal Army, because such sporting arms could easily be rebored to a larger size and adapted for military use. The Drafting Committee in Paris noted that these restrictions exceeded restrictions imposed on Austria by the treaty. The Conference of Ambassadors agreed. The only rule was that sporting arms must be of different calibre from that used by any European army.[30]

The hair-splitting decisions appropriate to various categories of war matériel were not applied to aeronautical matériel and equipment. Air clauses in the treaty were quite clear; all aeronautical equipment was to be considered suitable for combat, and must be confiscated or destroyed. That amounted to a considerable sacrifice for Austria. In December 1918, the *Volkswehr* had established a flying troop under the command of former Habsburg Captain Anton Silber. In January 1919 the organization of this tiny air force was fixed: command headquarters in Vienna supervised six air bases, each with an administrative and tactical unit, similar to a *Volkswehr* battalion. Airbases One and Two were in Wiener Neustadt, Three and Four in Graz-Thalerhof, and Five and Six in Vienna-Aspern. One group from Airbase Two operated in Klagenfurt, another in Salzburg. In April 1919 the Ministry of Transportation established a bureau for civil airborne travel that complemented the *Volkswehr* flying units.[31]

Although the Treaty of Saint Germain forbade all military aviation, Austria hoped to retain its cadre of pilots by using them in a police capacity. In February 1920, the Austrians requested that twenty airplanes be exempt from confiscation in order to be used as an aerial police force. The Conference of Ambassadors rejected the request, primarily on the grounds that a similar concession to Germany could be dangerous. The Allies noted that many airplanes in Germany needed only the reattachment of machine guns in order to serve as military weapons.[32]

The Austrians had no better luck in trying to retain military airfields for civilian use. The Aeronautical Control Commission

observed that Wiener Neustadt, well suited for military purposes, was of doubtful value for civil aviation because it was
situated fifty kilometers from Vienna. On the other hand, Aspern, only six kilometers from the capital, seemed destined to be
Vienna's airport. Graz, too, had some promise as a civil airport
on a line connecting Italy with Central Europe. Klagenfurt was
but a minor field, and other locations to the west were hardly
practical. Therefore, the Allies allowed only Aspern and Graz to
retain some of the existing buildings and equipment for use in
civil aviation.[33]

The controversy surrounding Austrian sales of airplanes and
associated aeronautical equipment paralleled the furor created
by Austrian export of war matériel. In fact, the Allied decision to
place Austrian depots under Allied control was primarily
motivated by alienation of aeronautical equipment. The Conference of Ambassadors received reports in May that a private
concern, called *Lufag (Luftfahrtwesen Gesellschaft),* had bought
aircraft matériel from the Austrian government and had sold it to
individuals in Austria, Poland, Czechoslovakia, and the
Ukraine.[34]

The question raised by these sales caused great consternation
among the Allies in Paris. In September 1920 the British provided information to the Conference of Ambassadors that indicated Austria had sold fifty-one Brandenburger airplanes to
Czechoslovakia through the intermediary of one Lieutenant
Kroeger. The powers directed Czechoslovakia to return the aircraft to the Allies, to whom the aircraft belonged.[35] Instructions
had been given in August 1920 to the Aeronautical Commission
to destroy all aeronautical matériel, but constant delays had prevented the action. In November further delays were ordred by
the Military Committee of Versailles as a result of Czechoslovak
claims on the matériel. On 24 November, the conference agreed
the sales were illegal, delivery of aeronautical matériel to
Czechoslovakia was forbidden, and matériel already in Czech
hands must be returned to the Aeronautical Control Commission
for destruction.[36]

In October 1920 the Aeronautical Control Commission reported to Paris that it was "powerless" to enforce the complete
aeronautical disarmament of Austria. The commission recommended indefinite suspension of civil aviation in Austria in order
to put pressure on the uncooperative Austrians. Foch's Military
Committee agreed and submitted a proposal to the Conference

of Ambassadors that extended indefinitely the three-month prohibition on manufacture or importation of aeronautical matériel.
The Conference of Ambassadors approved the proposal, which
stipulated that the Allies would fix the date when civil aeronautical activity could be resumed, a date dependent upon Austrian
compliance with the peace treaty.[37]

Frustrated with Austrian noncompliance, in October 1920 the
Inter-Allied Control Commissions announced intentions to remain in Austria longer than originally planned. Three months,
the Allies explained, had not been enough time to complete the
task of disarming Austria according to the treaty terms. Deutsch
disagreed and argued in a letter to Zuccari on 16 October that
Austria had fulfilled the treaty conditions. Deutsch claimed that
Austrian forces had been reduced and compulsory service abolished. He suggested that the few remaining difficulties regarding
war matériel would be handled by the Austrian ministry of com-
merce. Zuccari replied in an interview published in the *Neue
Freie Presse* on 22 October, claiming that Austrian obstruction
had been responsible for delays. The Allies could not get an
accurate count of war matériel from the Austrians and had to
conduct their own inventory. Zuccari remarked that Deutsch
himself could help the Control Commissions complete the task if
he would cooperate and provide an accurate count of war
matériel.[38]

Austrian obstruction certainly played a major role in delaying
completion of the required work. Deutsch's plan to cooperate as
little as possible, formulated in March 1920, served as the heart
of Austrian policy.[39] Deutsch managed to keep before the public
eye a picture of foreign generals on the *Ringstrasse*. On 12
November 1920, he publicly criticized the Control Commissions
in an address to the Austrian military union. Deutsch called for
the end of Allied control, because, he said, Austria had fulfilled
the treaty terms. He complained of the high cost, charging that
one hundred Allied officers cost the Austrian government more
than expenditures for the entire Austrian army.[40] Deutsch also
accused the Allies of bias against Austria; he remarked that
Allied concern about disarmament did not include Hungary, because the Entente was "mentally allied to agents of reaction" in
Horthy's regime.[41]

In December the Conference of Ambassadors took another
step in its attempt to force Austrian compliance with treaty
terms. The conference requested, in view of Austrian delays and

Lufag refusal to cooperate with the Aeronautical Control Commission, that Austria take three steps to demonstrate good intentions: (1) take legislative measures to ensure all aeronautical matériel on Austrian territory, no matter in whose hands, be handed over to the Aeronautical Control Commission; (2) cancel the *Lufag* contract made on 15 June 1919; and (3) take legislative action to prosecute and punish anyone in possession of aeronautical equipment that had not been declared to the Aeronautical Control Commission.[42]

Austria answered the Allied request on 30 December 1920 and on 6 January 1921. The Austrians maintained firmly that they had a right to dispose of war matériel—including aeronautical equipment—before 16 July 1920, when France ratified the treaty. Austria denied owing any indemnity for matériel transformed or sold before that date. The Conference of Ambassadors disagreed, but for the second time referred the question to a committee of jurists associated with the peace conference.[43]

Austrian resistance stiffened in part because Austrian officials had reason to hope in December 1920 that the Control Commissions would soon go home. A high French officer told an Austrian liaison officer that the Frenchman's family would be returning home in January 1921, and the French officer would need his living quarters only until mid-February. The Austrians assumed the Control Commissions would end their work by then.[44] The Austrian conclusion, however, was premature. In late January 1921, the Conference of Ambassadors was still undecided on the issue of terminating Allied control in Austria. The Italians and the British favored immediate dissolution of the Control Commissions. The French, however, led by Foch, opposed immediate dissolution, and even disapproved of setting a definite date for termination.

Foch described the problems remaining to be solved in Austria: assembled artillery matériel had yet to be distributed among the powers; some matériel, especially munitions, had yet to be recovered; police and "safety troops" had taken on an "abnormal" development that had to be restrained; and, finally, diverse irregular formations still flourished in Austria. The French representative Laroche added that if Hungary witnessed Allied toleration of incomplete Austrian disarmament, Hungary would be encouraged to seek the same situation. The ranking French diplomat, Cambon, noted that Eichoff himself (Austrian representative in Paris) had claimed the Control Commissions assisted the Austrian government in restraining the unruly army. The Conference of Ambassadors compromised by deciding to set 20 February 1921 as the date for dissolution of the Control Commissions, but to maintain in Austria a so-called Liquidation Organ to carry on the unfinished work of the Control Commissions.[45]

Italy disagreed with the other powers concerning details of the Liquidation Organ. The Conference of Ambassadors was told that Austria, expecting the Control Commissions to cease work on 20 February, had slackened her efforts to comply with Allied demands. Italy agreed with the other Allied powers that some sort of agency was necessary to carry on in place of the Control Commissions, but the Italian representative advocated a committee composed of military attachés whose cost would not fall on Austria. Britain opposed the use of attachés, but agreed to assume the cost of the British participation in the Liquidation Organ. The conference agreed to notify the Austrians that they must comply with the treaty, even though the Control Commissions would end their work in February; a Liquidation Organ would remain after 20 February to supervise compliance with the treaty.[46] Austria was notified of the decision just days before the Control Commissions were dissolved.[47]

Prospects for the new control mechanism received a severe setback on 17 February when the Conference of Ambassadors was informed that the Italian government had given instructions forbidding Italian participation in any sort of Inter-Allied Commission or Liquidation Organ after 20 February. Reacting to the news, Italy's allies argued that if Italy had her way, and all worked in their "own interests" instead of working in concert, the Treaty of Saint Germain would remain only partially executed. They feared a similar situation could easily develop in Germany. The impasse within the conference led to the unusual step of deciding by majority vote rather than unanimous consent that a Liquidation Organ of "military attachés or other officers" would be constituted; Italy reserved full liberty of action.[48] In early March 1921, the picture brightened somewhat when the Italian government authorized its attaché to collaborate temporarily and to participate in Allied meetings, now under the direction of General Hallier.[49]

Meanwhile, tension between the Allied representatives and the Austrians grew. The Austrian government published on 6 March 1921 the new constitution of the Liquidation Organ, whose senior officers were General Hallier and Colonel Barres (for aeronautical matters). The opposition Social Democrats (defeated in October 1920 elections) criticized the government for "subserviency" to the Allies. The government replied, with some justification, that Deutsch himself had begun the practice.[50] A continuing source of irritation and complaint concerned automobile accidents involving Allied cars and Austrian pedestrians.[51] Colonel Gosset, ranking British representative on the Liquidation Organ, revealed Allied exasperation when he expressed regret over an accident in May that caused slight injury to a child. Gosset noted recurring problems at tram stops, where the Austrian public exhibited a "lamentable disregard for passing traffic."[52]

Meanwhile, the jurists in Paris had returned an opinion in late January 1921 that once again supported the Allied interpretation on Austria's right to dispose of war matériel and aeronautical equipment. Shortly thereafter, a major controversy developed in connection with destruction of aeronautical equipment and buildings at Wiener Neustadt.

The Austrians were irate about reports that Allied officers had taken into their own hands the work of destruction so long advocated. On 15 February, Austrian press reports publicized an ugly incident at Wiener Neustadt between British Colonel Fletcher and a certain Herr Christian, an Austrian engineer. Fletcher reportedly reprimanded Christian for the slow pace of the work, seized the Austrian by the collar, and pushed him from the shed where equipment was supposed to be undergoing destruction. Workmen who witnessed the incident forced Fletcher to apologize, but new incidents fueled more indignation. On 17 February, one Captain Woodhouse and five British soldiers entered a propeller shed in Wiener Neustadt and began to demolish with axes the 4,000 propellers stored there. Workmen protested the action, but Woodhouse and his crew continued. Finally, the Austrian workmen threw themselves on the propellers, covering them with their bodies. The British group then quit attempts to destroy the equipment.[53]

After several Austrian objections and counterproposals to earlier directives, the newly formed Liquidation Organ demanded again immediate commencement of destruction. The Austrians gave up attempts to appeal to the control mechanisms in Vienna. Requests to various representatives of the Entente, the Austrians hoped, would induce the home governments to reverse the decision of the Liquidation Organ.[54] The Austrians were disappointed in their efforts to induce home governments to overrule the Liquidation Organ, but, on the other hand, the Liquidation Organ achieved little success in completing its task. The story throughout 1921 concerning aeronautical equipment was similar to problems relating to army war matériel. Hallier complained to the government of Austria with little result.[55] The Conference of Ambassadors in Paris continued to discuss Austrian intransigence, but always stopped short of threatening specific economic sanctions.[56]

The chief result, unfortunately, of Allied confiscation and destruction was to encourage hiding and hoarding of illegal arms. That was doubly unfortunate for the new republic, for the Austrians were arming against each other.

8

A House Divided

DEEP social and political rifts in Austrian society created a climate of domestic distrust and suspicion that unfortunately grew only more intense throughout the interwar period. Paramilitary groups associated with rival factions raised every political disagreement to a fever pitch, which threatened civil war. This regrettable situation grew out of the early years of the republic, when the Allies failed completely to effect the disarmament of the Austrian population.

In 1918, all kinds of self-help or self-defense organizations arose throughout Austria in response to the breakdown of governmental authority. Local towns and villages frequently armed themselves for protection against bands of soldiers from the Habsburg army. Deutsch had no objection to the organization of self-defense groups, and even hoped that such developments might lead to a future peoples' militia.[1] The ministry for military affairs frequently provided arms to various local groups. The self-help groups assumed a wide variety of names: *Bürgerwehr, Einwohnerwehr, Stadtwehr, Heimatdienst, Ortswehr, Bauernwehr, Heimwehr, Volkswehr, Selbstschutzverband, Heimatwehr, Heimatschutzverband,* and probably several others.[2]

Styria experienced one of the earliest transformations of volunteer bands into antisocialist organizations. In late 1918, a Social Democrat named Resel formed workers and peasants into guard units. Pressure from the Social Democratic Party, however, induced Resel to disband the peasant units and replace them with workers. The peasants reacted by seizing weapons and regrouping under new leaders. Several factions formed, which became, incidentally, an enduring characteristic and problem for the whole conservative *Heimwehr* movement in Austria throughout the interwar years. In this case, the factions gathered under the loose tacit leadership of the Christian Social governor of Styria, Anton Rintelen.[3]

The Styrian *Heimwehr* enjoyed a wealth of weapons and support, thanks to the Yugoslav threat. Peasants and students made up the bulk of the *Heimwehr,* which was led by former officers of the monarchy. Although *Vokswehr* officers occasionally assisted the local *Heimwehr* groups to acquire arms for defense against the common Yugoslav foe, the *Heimwehr* normally was criticized by the *Volkswehr.* The *Volkswehr* had reason for jealousy, since the *Heimwehr* acquired some 17,000 rifles, 236 machine guns, artillery, and even airplanes—much of it taken from *Volkswehr* depots in Styria.[4] The *Heimwehr* claimed to be nonpolitical, but socialists in the *Vokswehr* were not convinced. Rintelen himself was a Christian Social politician with strong German Nationalist leanings. His associates, including Schönerer's son-in-law and Dr. Walter Pfrimer in particular, all expressed fervent German nationalism and a dislike for socialism in any form. Even in early 1919, before anyone had heard of Hitler and National Socialism, it was impossible to regard as nonpolitical those battalions under Pfrimer that carried flags sporting the swastika and German colors. The student battalions had aims that went far beyond a nonpartisan defense of Austria: they advocated the "fight against Marxism and bourgeois democracy, [the] creation of an authoritarian state, and the *Anschluss.*" Peasant leaders were hardly less political, proclaiming support for "purely *völkisch* aims" including "the defense and regaining of German land and soil and the maintenance of law and order."[5]

From the beginning of the self-help phenomenon, the Tyrol was a leading center of *Heimwehr* activity. In November 1918, much like other towns threatened by disorder, Innsbruck organized a volunteer city militia. The leading organizer was Dr. Richard Steidle, who at the request of the Tyrolean National Council, began to set up new local groups in the spring of 1919 that were to collaborate with each other under the supervision of the provincial government. The short-lived Soviet regime in nearby Munich had stimulated the activity; from the start, the paramilitary groups in the Tyrol, oriented around traditional Tyrolean rifle clubs, had a strong anti-Communist, antisocialist raison d'être.[6]

The most dynamic self-defense activity in early 1919 took place in Carinthia against Yugoslav encroachments. In December 1918 the provisional government in Vienna became alarmed by the intentions of the Yugoslav commander, who planned to move his headquarters to Klagenfurt and station troops in other parts of Carinthia. Austria asked for American occupation of Klagenfurt and Villach to keep the Yugoslavs from effecting a fait accompli before the Paris Peace Conference met.[7] If the United States and its allies refused, the Austrians hoped for at least peaceful arbitration of the dispute.[8] Neither the request for Western occupation nor the hope for peaceful settlement were realized. Fighting continued, particularly around Völkermarkt (east of Klagenfurt), during the first six months of the year.[9] However, the *Volkswehr* participated actively in the fight along with local defense units. As a result, the *Heimatschutz* in Carinthia was the last of those in the Austrian *Heimwehr* movement to assume clearly bourgeois, partisan characteristics.[10]

Ironically, when the *Heimwehr* movement reached its peak in the late 1920s the organization concocted a legend that the Yugoslav fight marked a glorious highpoint and birthplace for the *Heimwehr*. In fact, in 1919 the Tyrolean *Heimwehr* had experienced a much greater degree of centralization and self-consciousness than the scattered bands in Carinthia and Styria.

The *Heimwehr* movement hardly represented all nonsocialist activities. As early as September 1919, some businessmen and nonsocialist employees formed councils of their own to counter soldiers' and workmen's councils.[11] By December, a so-called Citizens' Political League, oganized to protect conservative interests, had achieved sufficient status to cause concern among socialists. Armed *Volkswehr* men attempted to disrupt a meeting of the newly formed League on 1 December 1919, but succeeded only in prompting *Volkswehr* authorities to issue orders forbidding soldiers to carry arms in meetings. The Citizens' Political League provided fresh fuel for the socialist argument that the proletariat needed to arm itself for self-protection.[12]

An armed proletariat was no idle dream. Following the collapse of Béla Kun's Soviet regime in Hungary, Austrian Communists initiated a "drilling movement" involving armed workmen. The Communists began the movement in response to the Social

Democratic policy of cautious gradualism. Threats from the new reactionary regime in Hungary soon prompted socialist interest in the Austrian drilling movement, however, and the armed workmen quickly fell under Social Democratic domination. Particularly in Graz and in towns along the southern railway in Lower Austria, socialist groups recruited workers and conducted military exercises and drill. Deutsch claimed in February 1920 that not a single Worker Army *(Arbeiterwehr)* unit existed in Austria. Cuninghame reported that Deutsch's assertion was "only nominally true," as formed "bodies of workmen" were known to exist in a number of locations. The British attaché listed several examples, including 300 metal workers armed with automatic pistols at the Arsenal in Vienna, and "drilling groups" in Wiener Neustadt, Tirnitz, Gloggnitz, Neunkirchen, Bruck on the Mur, Graz, Leoben, and other Styrian mining towns. There were perhaps eight separate drilling groups in Graz, each attached to a particular factory in the area, and each possessing a machine gun detachment and several rifles. More arms were available in storage. Some estimates claimed as many as 8,000 participants in Graz. That figure, according to the ministry for military affairs, was too high, but the Austrian government had to admit that the correct figure was not known.[13]

More reports in March, eagerly publicized by the *Reichspost,* told of arms "issued" to some 700 workmen in Lower Austria who drilled as part of the Worker Army. Other reports claimed 300 rifles were distributed to workmen near Wiener Neustadt. In April, Bauer protested to Cuninghame that reports of armed workmen were greatly exaggerated, but Cuninghame nonetheless claimed that firm evidence supported charges that 2,200 workers at Tirnitz and Neunkirchen were involved in the Worker Army movement. They possessed 1,000 rifles and 32 machine guns, according to "reliable" reports.[14]

The socialists, of course, were not alone in organizing armed partisan groups. By 1920 the *Heimwehr* movement had developed a high level of self-consciousness and, thanks to right-wing regimes in Bavaria and Hungary, had accumulated a healthy supply of weapons. Right-wing groups in Bavaria, especially, cultivated extensive contacts with *Heimwehr* groups in Austria. A former German forester, Georg Escherich, emerged as leader of right-wing groups in Bavaria. Contact between Escherich's organization, the *Orgesch,* and *Heimwehr* leaders in Austria developed into a close relationship fostered by Rudolf

Kanzler, one of Bavaria's best organizers. Kanzler had proven his talent in Carinthia, where in late 1919 he played a crucial role in organizing and arming the Carinthian *Heimwehr.* He came in person on 28 February 1920 to witness the formal founding of the Salzburg *Heimwehr* organization. In March, Kanzler made contact with Steidle's *Heimwehr* group in the Tyrol, followed closely by liaison with *Heimwehr* leaders in Vorarlberg in the summer. Kanzler supplied not only organizational skill to Austrian groups, but convinced his financial backers in Bavaria to extend support to the Austrian formations.[15]

Any attempt to determine precise numbers regarding the size of the *Heimwehr* or the Worker Army is fraught with difficulty. An indication of their significance, however, especially in comparison to the Federal Army and Schober's police, can be seen by Kondert's estimate that by the end of 1920 the Austrian *Heimwehr* numbered about 100,000. Kondert credits the Worker Army with a membership of a similar size, plus superiority in arms, organization, and mobility vis-à-vis the conservative groups.[16] Given paramilitary forces of these dimensions, it is little wonder that politics became increasingly uneasy.

The Allies in Paris expressed early concern about the widespread possession of arms by peasants and workmen in Austria during the winter of 1919–20.[17] Allied representatives in Vienna, especially Lindley, urged the Conference of Ambassadors in Paris to press the Austrian government to disarm peasants and workmen, and have public and secret stores of arms delivered to the Allied powers. Foch relayed to the conference the concern shared by the Military Committee of Versailles that disarmament of the population proceed rapidly.[18]

Lieutenant Colonel Sir Thomas Cuninghame, the very astute British Military representative in Vienna since late December 1918, was a major driving force behind Entente concern about Austrian disarmament. General Segre had confined his concern to conditions of the armistice and to reduction of the official army, the *Volkswehr.* When Segre left Austria in January 1920, the British optimistically predicted that the new Italian commander would be more cooperative in facing the wider question of disarming the population.[19] Hopes for a quick solution to the disarmament problem led to a British initiative in Paris that prompted dispatch of advance echelons of the Inter-Allied Military Control Commissions. The Military Committee at Versailles under Marshal Foch endorsed wholeheartedly the British view that disarmament of the civil population and seizure of secret stores of arms in Austria was imperative.[20]

Official Austrian reaction to Allied entreaties was positive. Renner told Gosset in April that he intended to disarm the population by force if necessary, as soon as the Federal Army took shape.[21] Cuninghame, however, expressed skepticism. He noted the Austrian government hoped to disarm the people by exchanging surplus clothing and army equipment for arms, since cash payments would be too expensive. But, according to the British attaché, by April it was already too late. Delays in ratification of the treaty and postponement of the arrival of the Inter-Allied Control Commissions put the Austrian government in a very unfavorable position. The Kapp *Putsch* caused heightened suspicions in Austria and increased unwillingness to give up arms. Cuninghame argued that despite the government's wish to disarm the civilian populace, Vienna lacked the power to do so. Cuninghame advised the Control Commissions to work cautiously in cooperation with the Austrian government.[22] However, the time for cooperation had passed. Distrust and tension between the Allied Control Commissions and the Austrian government growing out of disagreements over the Federal Army and confiscation of war matériel naturally poisoned the atmosphere surrounding the question of civilian disarmament.

Abundant evidence could be found easily in the summer and autumn of 1920 that the population possessed dangerously large quantities of weapons. In June, Deutsch sounded an alarmist note in a conversation with Gosset. Deutsch warned that *Burgerwehr, Heimwehr,* and *Arbeiterwehr* formations threatened to plunge the country into civil war. Cuninghame and Lindley did not view the situation as critical, and observed that Deutsch's urging the Entente to disarm the private groups came as no surprise. Since the Federal Army was dominated by the Social Democrats, elimination of paramilitary groups would leave the socialists in control of the only significant force in the country.[23]

In November 1920 disputes between *Heimwehr* organizations and socialists came to a head in the Tyrol. Suspicion had blossomed in late October when a consignment of arms and ammunition from the Bavarian *Heimwehr* organization was seized at Innsbruck by a Social Democratic deputy and socialist railway workers.[24] A meeting of the Tyrol Rifle Association planned for 20 November provoked a strike by socialist railway workers.

The socialists charged that the original sporting character of the Rifle Association had been transformed into a reactionary political organization. The railway strike prevented Bavarian participation in the meeting, as it was designed to do, but only further enflamed subsequent partisan charges and countercharges.[25]

In December 1920 the Conference of Ambassadors turned its attention once again to the problem of disarming the civilian Austrian population. The Allied powers directed the Austrian government to disband irregular formations, and mentioned the *Heimwehr* and Worker Army specifically. The conference set a deadline for completion within two months, and threatened that noncompliance would result in the powers applying "such economic and financial pressure to bear as they may deem necessary."[26]

The Austrians, in the meantime, had promulgated a governmental decree that ordered surrender of all arms and ammunition owned or held by private individuals. The decree of 11 December 1920 set up special commissions to take custody of the equipment surrendered; compensation to owners would be settled by a special ordinance.[27]

Neither the decree nor the population's response met with Allied approval. In March, the Liquidation Organ asked for specific information on the special commissions and their progress. In addition, the Allies demanded to know why revolvers and pistols were not included in the disarmament decree.[28] The Austrians replied that commissions were set up in every province, with separate commissions for Vienna, Graz, and Wiener Neustadt. No information on progress was included in the reply. The Austrians explained somewhat lamely that revolvers and pistols did not fall under the purview of Saint Germain.[29] The Liquidation Organ quickly noted its dissatisfaction with the Austrian reply. The Allies believed a central commission was necessary, and demanded fortnightly reports on progress toward disarmament. A definite date must be set, said the Allies, for all arms to be turned in, including pistols.[30]

The program for disarming paramilitary groups was a failure. Throughout the spring of 1921, both right-wing and left-wing groups grew brazenly open about arming themselves, both citing the threat from the other side as justification. In March, Deutsch warned the Christian Socials of an extension of the program of arming workmen if the *Heimwehr* continued to develop. The conservatives replied that the Federal Army served as an instrument of the socialist party and the workmen, and the Christian Socials would defy attempts to disarm the *Heimwehr*.[31] On 24 March the *Arbeiter Zeitung* reported a meeting in Graz including Styrian bankers, manufacturers, and landowners. The socialist newspaper reported that the provincial Deputy Governor, a Christian Social, spoke of the need to develop and equip the *Heimwehr*, which he praised as an important Christian Social support. He requested two million crowns from the banks, two million from the manufacturers, and one million from the land-owners for support of the *Heimwehr*.[32] By June, few people denied the existence of paramilitary groups, and most admitted the influence of such groups was rising. The Allied Liquidation Organ found particularly offensive an article in the *Reichspost* on 23 June 1921 that freely discussed the various formations: *Arbeiterformationen, Selbstschutzverband, Frontkämpfervereinigung, Heimwehr, Arbeiterkolonie,* and the like.[33]

Allied disgust with the situation grew throughout the summer and autumn.[34] The Austrians protested in September that they had made efforts and accomplished all that was possible to dis arm the civilian populace. The Allied reply in October stated bluntly that words were not enough: energetic action must be undertaken. In December, the Allies flatly rejected an Austrian suggestion that most arms had been collected. The Liquidation Organ cited specific examples in Vorarlberg, Tyrol, Salzburg, and Wiener Neustadt. The Allies demanded the Austrian government pass a law with teeth in it to force disarmament in the country.[35]

The situation only became worse throughout 1922. Frequent Austrian claims to having solved the problem were disputed by the Liquidation Organ, only to have the matter referred time and again to Paris. The next dreary round would begin with a new series of Austrian promises, which grew progressively more difficult to keep.[36] Finally in April 1923, Deutsch and Körner showed the utter failure of disarmament efforts by publicly organizing the Republican Defense League, or *Schutzbund*. The path was set toward the bloody clashes of 1927 and the "Civil War" of 1934. The Allied Liquidation Organ stumbled along, unsuccessfully, until 1928 when the anachronism finally ceased operations.

A number of factors contributed to the failure of civilian disarmament. Paramilitary groups reflected a fatal flaw in Austrian democracy: rival groups harbored such suspicion of opponents that "rules of the game" usually associated with parliamentary government were disregarded by ideological enemies. This condition of Austrian political and social life provided the basic motive for the proliferation of paramilitary groups.

That is not to say civilian disarmament was impossible after the Great War—only very difficult. Immediate dispatch of Inter-Allied Control Commissions and a more cooperative Austrian response would have made disarmament more likely. Delay in French ratification of the peace treaty and Deutsch's policy of obstructionism, however, determined a different course of events.

Austria alone cannot be blamed, however, for delays in the completion of work by the Control Commissions. Once in place, the Control Commissions engaged in an unfortunate bureaucratic game of empire-building. The Allies insisted on strict literal interpretation of the treaty when it suited them, but resorted to arguments based on the "spirit of the treaty" at other times. No example is more trivial or ludicrous than the Austrian geographical mission to Brazil. Upon the invitation of the Brazilian government, a group of Austrian officers from the Military Geographical Institute in Vienna went to Brazil to assist in mapping the South American country. The Control Commissions in Austria induced the Conference of Ambassadors to request a recall of the "military mission" as a violation of the Treaty of Saint Germain.[37] (Article 158 prohibited Austria from sending military missions to other countries.) Brazil responded to the Conference of Ambassadors by noting that the Treaty of Saint Germain did not apply to Brazil, since Brazil had not been a signatory. Austria told the conference that the individuals who left for Brazil went as private citizens who had all resigned their military commissions.[38] In fact, the Geography Institute had been converted to a commercial enterprise before 1920. Officers and soldiers formerly assigned there worked as civilian employees.[39] After some deliberation, the Conference of Ambassadors eventually withdrew its demand for recall of the so-called military mission.

Another cause for delay in the Control Commission work was the unsettled condition of Austrian politics. The caretaker government without a chancellor, which served from the demise of the coalition in June 1920 until elections in October, could hardly be expected to respond to Control Commission directives with dispatch and energy. The October elections swept the Social Democrats from power, but the leading Christian Socials fell short of a majority. An attempt to form a government of "neutral" officials under Schober failed, so a Christian Social cabinet including several nonpolitical officials was formed on 20 November under the chancellorship of Dr. Michael Mayr. The ministry of military affairs was incorporated into the ministry of interior. The portfolio went to Baron Egon Glanz, one of the six nonparty officials in a cabinet of ten. In January 1921 the cabinet appointed Major General Rudolf Müller as permanent undersecretary of state in the ministry of interior, where he served briefly as head of army affairs.[40] In April a cabinet reshuffle once again separated army affairs from the ministry of interior.[41]

Only in 1922, with the emergence of Ignaz Seipel as the dominant political figure in Austria and Carl Vaugoin as the leading official responsible for military affairs did the new republic enjoy a stabilized political situation. By that time, interest in Western capitals about Austrian disarmament had waned considerably. Furthermore, Seipel and the Christian Socials soon incorporated the *Heimwehr*—for all practical purposes—into the very structure of Austrian government. By the mid-1920s it was simply too late to disband firmly entrenched paramilitary groups. Fear and suspicion that rivals might achieve a monopoly of force in the country guaranteed that no political group would give up the illegal arms upon which its security rested.

Notes

Preface

1. Austrians distinguish between the "first" Federal Army, 1920 to 1938, and the "second" Federal Army, 1955 to the present.

2. Ludwig Jedlicka, *Ein Heer im Schatten der Parteien: Die militärpolitische Lage Österreichs 1918–1938* (Graz, 1955).

3. C. Earl Edmondson, *The Heimwehr and Austrian Politics, 1918–1936* (Athens, Ga., 1978).

4. An unpublished dissertation touches peripherally on disarmament: Ursula Freise, "Die Tätigkeit der alliierten Kommissionen in Wien nach dem Ersten Weltkrieg," (Ph.D. diss., University of Vienna, 1963).

5. For example, Karl R. Stadler, *The Birth of the Austrian Republic, 1918–1921* (Leyden, 1966).

6. Nina Almond and Ralph Lutz, eds., *The Treaty of St. Germain: A Documentary History of Its Territorial and Political Clauses* (Stanford, Calif., 1935).

7. H. W. V. Temperley, ed., *A History of the Peace Conference of Paris* (London, 1921), 4: 141–57.

8. *Bericht über die Tätigkeit der deutschösterreichischen Friedensdelegation in St. Germain-en-Laye,* 2 vols. (Vienna, 1919).

Introduction

1. Title of a work by Hellmut Andics, *Der Staat den Keiner Wollte: Österreich 1918–1938* (Vienna, 1962).

2. The party name is confusing. The Christian Socials were by no means socialist.

3. Following the lead of Adam Wandruszka, this study uses the term *German Nationalists.* See Heinrich Benedikt, ed., *Geschichte der Republik Österreich* (Munich, 1954), pp. 289–485, for an excellent analysis of Austria's political structure by Wandruszka.

4. Otto Bauer, representing the left wing of the Social Democrats, made the observation at the end of October 1918 that the Austrian peasants, unlike the Russians, felt like members of the bourgeois class, and were determined enemies of the working class. Cited by F. L. Carsten, *Revolution in Central Europe, 1918–1919* (Berkeley, Calif., 1972), pp. 31–32.

5. Bruce F. Pauley, *The Habsburg Legacy 1867–1939* (New York, 1977), p. 167.

Chapter 1. Collapse of the Old Order

1. Gunther Rothenberg, "The Habsburg Army in the First World War: 1914–1918," in *The Habsburg Empire in World War I,* ed. Robert A. Kann, Béla K. Király, and Paula S. Fichtner (New York, 1977), p. 77.

2. Ibid., pp. 77–78.

3. Arthur J. May, *The Passing of the Hapsburg Monarchy, 1914–1918* (Philadelphia, 1966), 1:114.

4. May, *Passing of the Monarchy,* 2:796.

5. Karl Heinz, "Die Geschichte der österreichischen Arbeiterräte," from *Arbeitkammer* in Vienna, cited by Carsten, *Revolution,* p. 13; Charles A. Gulick, *Austria from Habsburg to Hitler* (Berkeley and Los Angeles, Calif., 1948), 1:41–42; Julius Deutsch, *Aus Österreichs Revolution: Militärpolitische Erinnerungen* (Vienna, n.d., ca. 1921), pp. 4–5; Gunther Rothenberg, *The Army of Francis Joseph* (Lafayette, Ind., 1976), p. 211.

6. Z. A. B. Zeman, *The Break-up of the Habsburg Empire, 1914–1918* (London, 1961), pp. 134–140, 219, 256.

7. Richard G. Plaschka, "Contradicting Ideologies: The Pressure of Ideological Conflicts in the Austro-Hungarian Army of World War I," in *The Habsburg Empire in World War I,* ed. Kann et al., p. 112.

8. Zeman, *The Break-up,* p. 143.

9. Ibid., pp. 143–46.

10. Ronald W. Hanks, "The End of An Institution: The Austro-Hungarian Army in Italy, 1918," (Ph.D. diss., Rice University, 1977), pp. 313–15, citing *Armeeoberkommando Secret Operations No. 1848* from the *Kriegsarchiv.* Not surprisingly, Ludendorff's self-serving memoirs recall a different version of high-level conversations in mid-August. Hanks argues persuasively that all parties—both emperors, Arz (Austrian chief of staff), Hindenburg, and Ludendorff—agreed that they could not win the war and that peace was imperative, although the Austrians believed the problem was more urgent than the Germans thought.

11. Edmund von Glaise-Horstenau, *The Collapse of the Austro-Hungarian Empire,* trans. I. F. D. Morrow (London, 1930), pp. 197–98; Otto Bauer, *The Austrian Revolution,* trans. H. J. Stenning (London, 1925), pp. 39, 45.

12. Ekengren (Swedish Minister) to Washington, 7 October 1918, printed in *FRUS,* 1918, Supp. 1, 1:341.

13. Glaise-Horstenau, *The Collapse,* pp. 197–98.

14. Victor S. Mamatey, *The United States and East Central Europe, 1914–1918: A Study in Wilsonian Diplomacy and Propaganda* (Princeton, N.J., 1957), p. 325.

15. Ibid., p. 335.

16. Lansing to Ekengren, 19 October 1918, printed in *FRUS,* 1918, Supp. 1, 1:368. Point Ten, expressed on 8 January 1918, had foreseen "autonomous" development for the peoples of the monarchy. Lansing explained that events since January had compelled the president to insist that the Czechoslovaks and Yugoslavs—not Wilson—be "judges of what action on the part of the Austro-Hungarian Government will satisfy their aspirations. . . ."

17. *StenProt, Prov. Nationalversammlung d.-österr.,* 21 October 1918.

18. Gulick suggests that the German Nationalists, or Pan-Germans, as he calls them, were "apparently intentionally unclear" as to whether the monarch would be Habsburg or Hohenzollern. (Gulick, *Habsburg to Hitler,* 1:54).

19. Fritz Fellner, ed., *Schicksalsjahre Österreichs 1908–1919: Das politische Tagebuch Josef Redlichs* (Graz, 1954), 2:310.

20. Klemens von Klemperer, *Ignaz Seipel: Christian Statesman in a Time of Crisis* (Princeton, N.J., 1972), pp. 84–85.

21. *StenProt, Prov. Nationalversammlung d.-österr.*, 30 October 1918.

22. Carsten, *Revolution*, pp. 26–29.

23. The provisional assembly in the Tyrol, for example, heavily Christian Social, sent a telegram to Vienna expressing preference for a republic.

24. *StRProt*, 11 November 1918.

25. The consensus among historians is that Ignaz Seipel, Catholic prelate and Christian Social politician, was mainly responsible for the wording of the document. For a good discussion and bibliographical guide to the somewhat clouded issue, see Klemperer, *Ignaz Seipel*, pp. 89–90.

26. *Neue Freie Presse*, 11 November 1918, afternoon ed., p. 1. (This translation by Gulick, *Habsburg to Hitler*, 1:60.)

27. *StenProt, Prov. Nationalversammlung d.-österr.*, 12 November 1918.

28. Deutsch, *Österreichs Revolution*, pp. 11–12.

29. Friedrich Funder, *From Empire to Republic* (New York, 1963), pp. 183–84.

30. Rothenberg, *Army of Francis Joseph*, p. 214.

31. *Österreich-Ungarns letzter Krieg, 1914–1918*, ed. *Österreichische Bundesministerium für Landesverteidigung* and the *Kriegsarchiv* (Vienna, 1938), 7:571–77.

32. Hanks, "End of An Institution," pp. 309–10.

33. Ibid., pp. 355–56.

34. Ibid., p. 351.

35. Rothenberg, *Army of Francis Joseph*, p. 217.

36. A. J. P. Taylor, *The Habsburg Monarchy, 1809–1918* (New York, 1965), p. 251.

37. Signed in London in 1915, the Treaty promised Italy considerable Habsburg territory in exchange for declaring war on Austria-Hungary.

38. *Letzter Krieg*, 7:577.

39. Hanks, "End of An Institution," p. 362.

40. "Protocol of the Armistice Between the Allied and Associated Powers and Austria-Hungary," in Sir Frederick Maurice, *The Armistices of 1918* (London, 1943), pp. 87–90.

41. Hanks, "End of An Institution," p. 366.

42. May, *Passing of the Monarchy*, 2:802.

43. Hanks, "End of An Institution," pp. 367–69.

44. Rothenberg, *Army of Francis Joseph*, p. 218.

45. Ibid. Rothenberg concludes the issue cannot be resolved.

46. Hanks, "End of An Institution," pp. 381–82.

47. Hanks's chapter title, invoking comparison to the more glorious phrase, "Drang nach Osten" (eastward expansion).

48. Rothenberg, *Army of Francis Joseph*, p. 220.

Chapter 2. Creation of the *Volkswehr*

1. *ZGBh, Fasz.* 2, Nr. 2, p. 4.

2. *StenProt, Prov. Nationalversammlung d.-österr.*, 30 October 1918; *StProt*, 30 October 1918.

3. *ZGBh. Fasz.* 2, Nr. 2, pp. 7–9.

4. Otto Bauer, *The Austrian Revolution*, trans. H. J. Stenning (London, 1925), p. 57.

5. *ZGBh, Fasz.* 2, Nr. 2, pp. 9–10; *Who's Who in Austria 1959/1960*, (Vienna, 1961), p. 90. Deutsch went on to serve as head of the private Social Democratic army—the

Schutzbund—from 1923 until 1934. He was a general in the Spanish Republican Army from 1936–39. He served in the New York office of war information from 1942–45 and returned to Austria in 1946. He died in 1968. (*Current Biography 1944*, pp. 152–54; *Current Biography 1968*, p. 454.)

6. Deutsch, *Österreichs Revolution*, pp. 1–9.

7. *StenProt, Prov. Nationalversammlung d.-österr.*, 30 October 1918; *StRProt*, 30 October, 31 October, 3 November 1918.

8. Karl Haas, "Studien zur Wehrpolitik der österreichischen Sozialdemokratie, 1918–1926," (Ph.D. diss., University of Vienna, 1967), pp. 11–18.

9. Deutsch, *Österreichs Revolution*, pp. 26–27.

10. *ZGBh, Fasz.* 2, Nr. 2, pp. 13–14.

11. *StRProt*, 8 November 1918; Haas, "Wehrpolitik," pp. 19–20.

12. Funder, *Empire to Republic*, p. 178.

13. An example of these appeals is a Swedish message to State, 14 November 1918, M-695, roll 5 (863.00/112).

14. *PdöW, Fasz:* "Oberbefehlshaber d.-österr. Wehrmacht," Nr. 138. Dated 15 December 1918, this document reflects guidelines *(Richtlinien)* issued 9 November.

15. *StRProt*, 5 and 7 November 1918.

16. *Verordnungsblatt d.-österr., StAfHW*, Nr. 1, 15 November 1918.

17. *ZGBh, Fasz.* 2, Nr. 2, pp. 25–26.

18. *PdöW, Fasz:* "Oberbefehlshaber d.-österr. Wehrmacht," Nr. 138.

19. Deutsch, *Österreichs Revolution*, pp. 28ff, 49ff; Bauer, *Revolution*, pp. 49ff.

20. Haas, "Wehrpolitik," p. 29.

21. *Arbeiter Zeitung*, 9 November 1918.

22. *ZGBh, Fasz.* 2, Nr. 2, pp. 35–36.

23. Jedlicka, *Ein Heer*, p. 14.

24. *StRProt*, 13 November 1918; Haas, "Wehrpolitik," p. 37.

25. Erwin Steinböck, *Die Volkswehr in Kärnten unter Berücksichtigung des Einsatzes der Freiwilligenverbände* (Vienna, 1963), p. 9.

26. *StRProt*, 9 December 1918.

27. Steinböck, *Volkswehr in Kärnten*, p. 9.

28. *PdöW, Fasz:* "Oberbefehlshaber d.-österr. Wehrmacht," Nr. 444, Nr. 444/1.

29. Haas, "Wehrpolitik," pp. 40–42.

30. Anna Eisenmenger, *Blockade: The Diary of an Austrian Middle-Class Woman, 1914–1924* (New York, 1932), p. 80.

31. Bauer, *Revolution*, p. 58.

32. Deutsch's tactics reflected the general socialist policy, described succinctly by Cuninghame as "always seeming to concede to the demands of the 'Left' but in appearance only." (Cuninghame to Twiss, 1 July 1919, printed in *DBFP*, 6:5.)

33. For example, although he says the *Volkswehr* was of "no use" in foreign policy or in maintaining internal order, Glaise-Horstenau adds that it served admirably to neutralize "many wild spirits, dangerous not only in a political but in a criminal sense." (*Collapse*, p. 322.)

34. Julius Deutsch, *Ein weiter Weg* (Vienna, 1960), pp. 118–19.

35. *StRProt*, 11 November 1918; Haas, "Wehrpolitik," pp. 25–27.

36. Manfried Rauchensteiner and Erwin Pitsch, *Die Stiftskaserne in Krieg und Frieden* (Vienna, 1977), pp. 53–54; Gerhard Botz, *Gewalt in der Politik* (Munich, 1976), pp. 32–36.

37. Vienna Police reports on 25 January 1919 recorded Kisch's claims to having 4,000 followers among the soldiers who were ready for revolution and the establishment of a socialist republic on their own terms. Cited by Carsten, *Revolution*, p. 87.

38. Eisenmenger, *Blockade*, p. 96.

39. *StAfHW* to *Oberbefehlshaber*, 26 November 1918, *PdöW, Fasz:* "Oberbefehlshaber," Nr. 285.

40. Bauer, *Revolution*, p. 85.

41. *Volkswehrkommando Kreis B* to *Volkswehrkommando Wien*, 28 December 1918 and 22 January 1919, *PdöW, Fasz.* 11 and 21, cited by Carsten, *Revolution*, p. 32.

42. These figures include officers but do not include those who served without arms in the support of service companies *(Hilfsdienstabteilungen)*. Figures from *ZGBh, Fasz.* 2, Nr. 2, p. 44.

43. Carsten, *Revolution*, p. 84.

44. Coolidge to Paris, 10 January 1919, printed in *FRUS-PPC*, 2:229.

45. Coolidge to Paris, 20 March 1919, printed in *FRUS-PPC*, 12:280.

46. Ibid.

47. Eisenmenger, *Blockade*, pp. 164–65.

48. *Reichspost*, 29 December 1918.

49. BAFR, 7 April 1920, F.O. 371/3537 (191478); Glaise-Horstenau, *Collapse*, p. 321.

50. Biographical details from Gerald Kleinfeld, "Stabilization and Reconstruction in Austria: Schober and Seipel, 1921–1922," (Ph.D. diss., New York University, 1961), pp. 35–41.

51. Schober's sympathies in 1918 were close to the Christian Social position, but he was regarded as a politically neutral civil servant. He served briefly as head of a nonpolitical "Government of Bureaucrats" in 1921–1922. He played a more controversial role as chancellor in 1929–1930; the "Schober bloc" consisted of an amalgam of the Agrarian League and the German Nationalists, opposed by Christian Socials and Social Democrats, but supported (however briefly) by the *Heimwehr* movement. Schober achieved success in 1930 in getting the signatories of St. Germain to renounce all claims to reparations and to the mortgage of Austria's wealth. The Christian Socials and the disillusioned *Heimwehr* sabotaged his government in late 1930. Schober died in 1932.

52. Coolidge Report, 9 February 1919, M-820, roll 9 (purport listing), 184.01102/76.

53. Friedrich Austerlitz, editor of the socialist *Arbeiter Zeitung,* provides an accurate barometer of socialist opinion. In April 1919 he admitted to a member of the American Coolidge Mission that the Austrian government could not control the *Volkswehr,* but he argued that the *Volkswehr* was not dangerous. The *Volkswehr* men are chiefly good (socialist) Viennese citizens, said Austerlitz, interested in maintaining public order and "the good wages and living which the members enjoy as compared with other occupations." (Bundy to Coolidge, 10 April 1919, printed in *FRUS-PPC*, 12:290–91.)

54. Ingrun Lafleur, "Socialists, Communists and Workers in the Austrian Revolution 1918–1919," (Ph.D. diss., Columbia University, 1972), p. 195.

55. Robert Hoffmann, "The British Military Representative in Vienna, 1919," *Slavonic and East European Review* 52 (1974): 265–66.

56. Julius Braunthal to Karl Haas, 19 November 1964, cited by Haas, "Wehrpolitik," p. 28.

57. *Verordungsblatt d.-österr. StAfHW,* Nr. 1, 15 November 1918.

58. Jonathan Zorach, "The Czechoslovak Army, 1918–1938," (Ph.D. diss., Columbia University, 1975), p. 152.

59. On 31 December 1918, Vorarlberg: 948; Tyrol: 2460; Salzburg: 1946. Figures include officers. From *ZGBh, Fasz.* 2, Nr. 2, p. 44.

60. Carsten, *Revolution*, p. 94.

61. Ibid., p. 95.

62. Eisenmenger, *Blockade, passim.*

63. Carsten, *Revolution*, p. 92; Botz, *Gewalt in der Politik*, pp. 41–42.

64. Carsten, *Revolution*, p. 91.

65. Julius Braunthal, *The Tragedy of Austria* (London, 1948), p. 72. Braunthal was Deutsch's adjutant, and a prominent Social Democrat.

66. For details, see Steinböck, *Volkswehr in Kärnten* and *Die Kämpfe in Raum Völkermarkt 1918/1919* (Vienna, 1969). For background, see Claudia Kromer, *Die Vereinigten Staaten von Amerika und die Frage Kärnten 1918–1920* (Klagenfurt, 1970), and Ivo J. Lederer, *Yugoslavia at the Paris Peace Conference: A Study in Frontiermaking* (New Haven, Conn., 1963). Reports from the American Lieutenant Colonel Miles and Lieutenant King to Coolidge from Carinthia are printed in *FRUS-PPC*, 12:468–523.

67. Carsten, *Revolution*, pp. 97–98.

Chapter 3. Between Left and Right

1. *StenProt Konst. Nationalversammlung d.-österr.*, 1:97, cited by Klemens von Klemperer, "Austria, 1918–1920: Revolution by Consensus," *Orbis* 10 (1967): 1071.

2. *KabProt*, 28 and 29 November 1918.

3. Steinböck, *Volkswehr in Kärnten*, pp. 7–8; Haas, "Wehrpolitik," p. 49.

4. Deutsch, *Österreichs Revolution*, pp. 82ff; Jedlicka, *Ein Heer*, pp. 18ff.

5. Numerous studies can be found in the *Kriegsarchiv*, for example, *ZGBh, Fasz. 2*, Nr. 1 and Nr. 4, and *Fasz. 6*. The *Kriegsarchiv* library has an unpublished paper by Friedrich Weber, "Die Planungen des Deutsch-Österreichischen Staatsamtes für Heerwesen zur Aufstellung einer bewaffneten Macht vor Wirksamwerden der Bestimmungen des Friedensvertrages von St. Germain in den Jahren 1918 und 1919" (*Militärwissenschaftliche Arbeit*, Vienna, 1978).

6. Coolidge to Paris, 7 April 1919, printed in *FRUS-PPC*, 12:286.

7. Coolidge to Paris, second dispatch dated 7 April 1919, printed in *FRUS-PPC*, 12:287–88.

8. PPC-DB, No. 94, dated 6 May 1919 (Hoover Institution).

9. Botz, *Gewalt in der Politik*, pp. 43–45.

10. Ibid., p. 45.

11. Alfred D. Low, "The First Austrian Republic and Soviet Hungary," *Journal of Central European Affairs* 20 (1960): 183.

12. See, for example, Coolidge Reports dated 14 and 15 April 1919, M-820, roll 9 (purport listing), 184.01102/346 and 354.

13. Of the many accounts of the Holy Thursday incident, the best and most detailed is Botz, *Gewalt in der Politik*, pp. 43–53.

14. Botz, *Gewalt in der Politik*, p. 50.

15. Gulick, *Habsburg to Hitler*, 1:76.

16. Lafleur, "Socialists," p. 311.

17. Except where otherwise indicated, the preceeding details from Botz, *Gewalt in der Politik*, pp. 50–52.

18. Bauer, *Revolution*, p. 105.

19. Bundy to Coolidge, 19 April 1919, printed in *FRUS-PPC*, 12:306.

20. *Reichspost*, 18 April 1919, quoted by Gulick, *Habsburg to Hitler*, 1:77.

21. Low, "Austrian Republic and Soviet Hungary," p. 184.

22. Coolidge to Paris, 19 April 1919, M-820, roll 9 (purport listing), 184.01102/380.

23. It is revealing that immediately after his description and analysis of the Thursday *Putsch*, Botz entitles the next two sections of his study "The Beginning of the Counter-

Revolution" and "Increase in Communist Agitation." (*Gewalt in der Politik*, pp. 53–55.)

24. An account sympathetic to Serge can be found in David F. Strong, *Austria (October 1918–March 1919): Transition from Empire to Republic* (New York, 1939), pp. 214–40. Strong relies heavily on Segre's own account (*Le missione militare italiana per l'armistizio*). Bauer, on the other hand, misses no opportunity in his *Austrian Revolution* to criticize Segre. Freise gives a somewhat more balanced account in her rather general and incomplete description in "Die Tätigkeit der alliierten Kommissionnen."

25. Armistice terms stipulated that the items in question remain *in situ.* (Maurice, *Armistices of 1918*, p. 88.)

26. *The New York Times,* 18 February 1919, p. 1.

27. The removal of art treasures exceeded provisions of the armistice and the future peace treaty. The Italian action prompted criticism from Italy's western allies; the confiscation quickly came to a halt, although Austrian press criticism continued into April. Italy made some effort in August and September to sign a separate treaty with Austria allowing retention of the seized booty. Renner refused. (Coolidge to Paris, 17 and 18 April 1919, M-820, roll 9, purport listing, 184.01102/367 and 377; Halstead to State, 15 September and 12 December 1919, printed in *FRUS-PPC*, 12:571 and 605.)

28. Freise, "Die Tätigkeit," p. 6.

29. Deutsch to American Attaché in Berne, 17 March 1919, *NPA Karton* 322, folio 651–52.

30. *ZGBh, Fasz.* 2, Nr. 2, p. 48.

31. Coolidge to Paris, 23 April 1919, M-820, roll 9 (purport listing), 184.01102/392.

32. *StAfHW* directive, 4 May 1919, *NPA Karton* 328, folio 36. Most secondary accounts of the Italian demand give the misleading impression that the requirement was for a 25 percent reduction in the *Volkswehr.* In fact, the demand amounted to a reduction of more than 60 percent.

33. Thirty battalions accounted for 12,000 men; technical troops, cavalry, artillery, other specialties, and higher command organizations accounted for 8,000. (Freise, "Die Tätigkcit," p. 6 n. 4)

34. *StAfHW* directive, 4 May 1919, *NPA Karton* 328, folio 38, p. 5.

35. Coolidge to Paris, 7 April 1919, printed in *FRUS-PPC*, 12:286.

36. Haas, "Wehrpolitik," pp. 52–54.

37. Low, "Austrian Republic and Soviet Hungary," p. 187.

38. Lafleur, "Socialists," p. 334.

39. Freise, "Die Tätigkeit," p. 7.

40. Bauer, *Revolution,* p. 107.

41. Lafleur, "Socialists," p. 344.

42. The high proportion of youth, women, and disabled soldiers in the crowd prompted subsequent Social Democrat accusations that the Communists sent the young and the feeble to do their work. (Lafleur, "Socialists," p. 349.)

43. Botz, *Gewalt in der Politik,* pp. 64–70; Lafleur, "Socialists," pp. 342–59; Bauer, *Revolution,* pp. 107–9; Halstead to Paris, 17 June 1919, printed in *FRUS-PPC*, 12:532–33.

44. Lafleur is the exception, arguing that the Communist movement could have been more successful had the Social Democrats not been so conservative. She fails to support her argument, however.

45. Botz, *Gewalt in der Politik,* p. 68.

46. Bauer, *Revolution,* p. 109.

47. Ibid.

48. Botz, *Gewalt in der Politik,* pp. 70–74.

49. Halstead to State, 5 Sep 1919, printed in *FRUS-PPC,* 12:564.

50. Kondert, "Heimwehr," pp. 9–12. See chap. 8 of this study for discussion of Heimwehr.

51. Halstead to State, 1 July, 5 September, and 13 September 1919, M-820, roll 9 (purport listing), 184.011102/82, 410, 445, and 447; also, 5 September 1919, printed in *FRUS-PPC,* 12:563. Halstead was not a very astute observer; a comparison of his reports with Cuninghame's reveals a two- to three-month lag in Halstead's correct assessment of developments. Halstead's reports, unlike Coolidge's, must be used only with the greatest circumspection.

52. Cuninghame to Twiss, 1 July and 8 July 1919, printed in *DBFP,* 6:5–8 and 37–38.

53. Ibid., 8 July 1919.

54. BAFR, 7 April 1919, F.O. 371/3537 (191478).

55. Carsten, *Revolution,* p. 90.

Chapter 4. Decision in Paris

1. Exchange of notes in *Bericht über die Tätigkeit,* 1:17–20, printed in Almond and Lutz, *Treaty,* pp. 39–41.

2. C.F., 8 May 1919.

3. Summary of Supreme War Council meeting held 11 May 1919, in Temperley, *Peace Conference,* 4:144–45. There was sympathy for the Austrian position in lower echelons of representatives from all countries. American Colonel Grant reported that a number of the military representatives were of the opinion that an injustice was being done in forcing Austria to maintain a volunteer army, but the military authorities were obliged "to follow the precedent set in the German Treaty." (Steering Committee Minutes, 5 August 1919, printed in *FRUS-PPC,* 11:475.)

4. C.F., 15 May 1919.

5. Ibid.

6. The chief advocate of this line of argument was Lloyd George. The most significant of those holding the opposite view was Marshal Foch.

7. Ibid.

8. Figures were: Austria—40,000; Hungary—45,000; Bulgaria—20,000; Czechoslovakia—50,000; Yugoslavia—40,000; Rumania—60,000; Poland—80,000; and Greece—20,000. Germany's limit had already been fixed at 100,000. (C.F., 23 May 1919, A.M.)

9. C.F., 23 May 1919 (P.M.).

10. C.F., 26 May 1919 (P.M.).

11. Renner to Clemenceau, 24 May 1919, printed in Almond and Lutz, *Treaty,* p. 43.

12. C.F., 26 May 1919 (A.M. & P.M.); C.F., 27 May 1919 (A.M.).

13. President of the Peace Conference (Clemenceau) to Renner, 27 May 1919, printed in Almond and Lutz, *Treaty,* pp. 44–45.

14. C.F., 27 May 1919 (A.M.).

15. For general background on French and Italian interests in Central Europe, see: Piotr S. Wandycz, *France and Her Eastern Allies, 1919–1925* (Minneapolis, Minn., 1962); René Albrecht-Carrié, *Italy at the Peace Conference* (Hamden, Conn., 1966); Arno J. Mayer, *Politics and Diplomacy of Peacemaking: Containment and Counterrevolution at Versailles, 1918–1919* (New York, 1967).

16. C.F., 29 May 1919 (A.M.).

17. Minutes, plenary session, 29 May 1919, printed in Almond and Lutz, *Treaty,* pp. 61–64.

18. Minutes, plenary session, 2 June 1919, printed in Almond and Lutz, *Treaty,* pp. 61–64. Portions of the military terms were included.

19. Ibid.

20. C.F., 4 June 1919 (P.M.).

21. C.F., 5 June 1919 (P.M.).

22. Ibid.

23. Exchange of notes on this subject printed in Almond and Lutz, *Treaty,* pp. 68–71.

24. Austrian comments were submitted 6 August 1919. Reply to these "counter-proposals" dated 11 August 1919, in M-820, roll 381 (185.215/13). English-language version, 185.2151/28, dated 12 August 1919.

25. *StAfHW* to *StAfA,* 25 July 1919, *NPA Karton* 374, folio 435–41; Austrian comments on "Clauses militaires, navales, et aériennes," *NPA Karton* 376, folio 206–10.

26. Summary of Supreme War Council meeting held 11 August 1919, in Temperley, *Peace Conference,* 4:153.

27. H.D., 25 August 1919.

28. This article and all that follow are from the Treaty of Saint Germain.

29. Temperley, *Peace Conference,* 4:147.

30. "Note to Austrian Delegation Accompanying Final Peace Conditions," 2 September 1919, printed in Almond and Lutz, *Treaty,* pp. 225–31.

31. H.D. 60, 25 September 1919; H.D. 68, 11 October 1919.

32. "Munitions, Armament, Material and Fortifications."

33. "Establishments, Recruiting and Military Training."

34. H.D. 68, 11 October 1919.

35. C.A., 14 February 1920.

Chapter 5. Echoes in Vienna

1. Hallier to [French] Minister of War, 3 August 1919, M-820, roll 381 (185.2151/25).

2. Ibid.

3. Halstead to State, 15 September 1919, printed in *FRUS-PPC,* 12:573.

4. DuBois to State, 9 October 1919, M-695, roll 21 (863.20/2).

5. Haas, "Wehrpolitik," pp. 104–5.

6. Cuninghame to Oliphant, 17 October 1919, printed in *DBFP,* 6:299. Schumpeter had failed to provide even a plan, however futile, to save the Austrian currency.

7. DuBois to State, 18 October 1919, printed in *FRUS-PPC,* 12:580–84.

8. Ibid.

9. Jedlicka, *Ein Heer,* p. 22. The fear of reaction dominated Social Democratic arguments. Deutsch argued in party circles that the socialists must remain in government until an army law was passed and a new army built, in order to insure protection of the republican form of government from the forces of reaction. (Haas, "Wehrpolitik," p. 108.)

10. Lindley to Curzon, 1 December 1919, and Curzon to Lindley, 15 December 1919, printed in *DBFP,* 6:454–55 and 514.

11. BAFR, 21 January 1920, F.O. 371/3534 (178647).

12. BAFR, 3 February 1920, F.O. 371/3534 (178580).

13. BAFR, 17 February 1920, F.O. 371/3535 (181524).

14. BAFR, 15 March 1920, F.O. 371/3536 (189157).

15. BAFR, 15 March 1920, F.O. 371/3536 (189157).

16. Ibid. (A conference to settle the federal issue was scheduled for 14 April at Linz.)

17. Ibid.

18. BAFR, 27 March 1920, F.O. 371/3536 (190001).

19. Enclosure, DuBois to State, 10 April 1920, M-695, roll 21 (863.20/3).

20. Halstead requested and received a report on the "Austrian Military Situation" from an unnamed "leading conservative in Austria." The highly partisan report provides a distorted interpretation of facts, but does portray vividly the conservative mood in 1920. Report enclosed in Halstead to State, 23 June 1920, M-695, roll 21 (863.20/6).

21. Details from BAFR: 21 January 1920, F.O. 371/3534 (178647); 3 February 1920, F.O. 371/3534 (178580); 15 March 1920, F.O. 371/3536 (189157); 26 March 1920, F.O. 371/3536 (190001).

22. BAFR, 21 January 1920, F.O. 371/3534 (178647).

23. BAFR, 15 March 1920, F.O. 371/3536 (189157).

24. BAFR: 15 March 1920, F.O. 371/3536 (189157); 27 March 1920, F.O. 371/3536 (190001); 6 April 1920, F.O. 371/3536 (190802).

25. In Vienna, one bureau was for the city, one for Lower Austria outside the city, and one for the Burgenland, where no recruiting would be possible until settlement of the dispute with Hungary for possession of the province.

26. BAFR: 15 March 1920, F.O. 371/3536 (189157); 6 April 1920, F.O. 371/3536 (190802 and 190803).

27. BAFR: 1 April 1920, F.O. 371/3536 (190799); 10 April 1920, F.O. 371/3537 (193648).

28. Gosset (ICC) to War Office, 24 April 1920, F.O. 371/3537 (194440).

29. Cuninghame to Lindley, 6 May 1920, F.O. 371/3538 (198049).

30. Deutsch to provincial governments, 20 March 1920, found in F.O. 371/3538 (201945).

31. BAFR: 6 April 1920, F.O. 371/3536 (190803); 22 May 1920, F.O. 371/3538 (201947).

32. BAFR: 18 June 1920, F.O. 371/4643 (file number unclear); 6 July 1920, F.O. 371/4643 (C-1667); 11 August 1920, F.O. 371/4643 (C-4318). See also Nicholson to Bridgeman, 12 September 1920, F.O. 371/4643 (C-7338).

33. Raymond E. Bell, Jr., "A Unionized Army in Battle: The Burgenland Action," *History, Numbers and War* 1 (1977): 183; Halstead to State, 28 May 1920, M-695, roll 21 (863.20/4) includes the constitution and bylaws of the union; also, BAFR, 6 June 1920, F.O. 371/3538 (20453).
The Front Veterans Association was not a trades union in any normal sense, but grew out of earlier mutual aid associations for officers. The Front Veterans Association held its first plenary session on 30 May 1920, and proclaimed intentions to assist less fortunate exofficers. That was only a cover for the real purpose, which was counterrevolutionary, anti-Semitic agitation. The organization included exofficers and welcomed any non-Jewish person opposed to socialism, regardless of service at the front. (Kondert, "Heimwehr," pp. 27–30.)

34. C. A. Macartney, *The Social Revolution in Austria* (Cambridge, 1926), p. 139. Macartney's sojourn in the new republic after 1918 makes his account that of an astute eyewitness. See also Jedlicka, *Ein Heer,* pp. 22, 30–31.

35. Conversation reported in Lindley to Curzon, 19 June 1920, F.O. 371/3538 (205422).

36. BAFR: 15 March 1920, F.O. 371/3536 (189157); 10 April 1920, F.O. 371/3537 (193648); 9 May 1920, F.O. 371/3538 (198518).

37. BAFR: 10 April 1920, F.O. 371/3537 (193648), and 9 May 1920, F.O. 371/3538 (198518).

38. Lindley to Curzon, 9 April 1920, F.O. 371/3537 (191478).

39. BAFR: 22 May 1920, F.O. 371/3538 (201947); 30 May 1920, F.O. 371/3538 (201946).

40. Funder, *Empire to Republic*, p. 228. (Funder incorrectly places the debate on 11 June.)

41. Cuninghame to Lindley, 5 June 1920, F.O. 371/3538 (204535).

42. BAFR, 18 June 1920, F.O. 371/4643 (file number unclear).

43. BAFR, 18 June 1920, F.O. 371/4643 (file number unclear).

44. Funder, *Empire to Republic*, p. 228.

45. Lindley to Curzon, 11 June 1920, printed in *DBFP*, 12:197–98; BAFR, 18 June 1920, F.O. 371/4643 (file number unclear).

46. Klemperer, "Austria, 1918–1920," p. 1077; BAFR, 6 July 1920, F.O. 371/4643 (C-1667).

47. BAFR, 18 June 1920, F.O. 371/4643 (file number unclear).

48. Klemperer, *Seipel*, pp. 136–45; BAFR, 11 August 1920, F.O. 371/4643 (C-4318); Nicholson to Bridgeman, 12 September 1920, F.O. 371/4643 (C-7338).

49. BAFR, 21 August 1920, F.O. 371/4643 (C-5416).

50. Lindley to Curzon, 10 July 1920, printed in *DBFP*, 12:222–23.

Chapter 6. The Army of Saint Germain

1. Excerpt from Halstead report, 7 December 1919, M-820, roll 382 (185.2154/13).

2. *StAfHW* to *StAfA*, 23 January 1920, and *StAfA* to Eichoff, 27 January 1920, Z. 268/Abt., *NPA Karton* 388.

3. Eichoff to Clemenceau, 3 February 1920 (Appendix F to C.A., 14 February 1920); BAFR, 16 February 1920, F.O. 371/3535 (181524).

4. C.A., 14 February 1920.

5. Deutsch to Renner, 13 March 1920, and Renner to Deutsch, 14 March 1920, Z. 1080/Fra, *NPA Karton* 366.

6. Deutsch to Renner, ca. 23 March 1920, Z. 1167/Fra, *NPA Karton* 366. Deutsch's words: "Uebrigens glaube ich, dass wir uns einen gewissen Einfluss auf die Art und das Tempo der Arbeiten der Ausschüsse unschwer sichern können."

7. BAFR, 9 May 1920, F.O. 371/3538 (198518).

8. Brig. Gen. Cavalerro to Gen. Weygand, 30 May 1920, included in C.A., 5 June 1920 (P.M.).

9. C.A., 19 June 1920.

10. *StAfA* to *StAfHW* et al., 26 June 1920, Z. 2577/Fra, *NPA Karton* 366; *StAfA* to Eichoff, 3 July 1920, Z. 2610/Fra, *NPA Karton* 366.

11. BAFR, 9 November 1920, F.O. 371/4644 (C-11812).

12. C.A., 25 June 1920.

13. *NPA Karton* numbers 366-67, passim.

14. BAFR, 12 September 1920, F.O. 371/4643 (C-7338).

15. C.A., 12 April 1920.

16. C.A., 4 May 1920.

17. Temperley, *Peace Conference*, 4:156–57.

18. *Bericht über die Tätigkeit des Heeresüberwachungsausschusses*, 1 May 1921, Z. 1936/Fra, *NPA Karton* 367.

19. Ibid., 1 May 1921, Z. 1936/Fra, *NPA Karton* 367.

20. C.A., 5 June 1920.

21. Zuccari to Austrian government, 5 May 1920, Z. 2196/Fra, *NPA Karton* 326.

22. *StAfHW* to *StAfA*, 18 (or 28) May 1920, Z. 2196/Fra, *NPA Karton* 326.

23. C.A., 5 June 1920.

24. *StAfA* to Eichoff, 15 June 1920, Z. 2383/Fra, *NPA Karton* 326.

25. *StAfHW* to *StAfA*, 30 June 1920, Z. 2627/Fra, *NPA Karton* 326, includes a letter of explanation from Zuccari to Hallier; see also telegram Eichoff to *StAfA*, 2 July 1920, Z. 2629/Fra, *NPA Karton* 326.

26. Eichoff to *StAfA*, 23 August and 30 August 1920, Z. 3568/Fra and Z. 3661/Fra, *NPA Karton* 326.

27. C.A., 20 October 1920.

28. Zuccari to *StAfHW* and *StAfA*, 4 November 1920, NPA Karton 326.

29. Hallier to *BMfHW*, 17 November 1920, included in *BMfHW* to *BMfA* 11 December 1920, Z. 5195/Fra, *NPA Karton* 326.

30. C.A., 15 December 1920.

31. Hallier to *BMfHW*, 4 January and 22 January 1921, Z. 378/Fra, *NPA Karton* 326.

32. BAFR, 17 February 1921, F.O. 371/5747 (C-4737).

33. Liq. Org. to Mayr, 21 March 1921, Z. 1132/Fra, *NPA Karton* 326.

34. Liq. Org. to Mayr, 31 March 1921, Z. 1285/Fra, *NPA Karton* 326: "Il est impossible d'amettre qu'en l'espace de deux mois le Gouvernment autrichien n'ait pu disposer du temps nécessaire au vote des Lois en question."

35. *BMfHW* to Liq. Org., 15 April 1921, Z. 1537/Fra, *NPA Karton* 326.

36. BAFR, 26 May 1921, F.O. 371/5747 (C-12270).

37. Liq. Org. to *BMfHW*, 16 March 1921, Z. 1015/Fra, *NPA Karton* 326.

38. BAFR, 9 July 1921, F.O. 371/5747 (C-15583).

39. Liq. Org. to *BMfA*, 1 August 1921, Z. 3638/Fra, *NPA Karton* 326.

40. Liq. Org. to *BMfA*, 16 September 1921, Z. 4760/Fra, *NPA Karton* 326, cites Austrian letter of 10 August.

41. Hallier to Foch, 22 August 1921, and Foch to Hallier, 7 September 1921, enclosures in report to State, 23 November 1921, M-695, roll 21 (863.20/10).

42. Liq. Org. to *BMfA*, 16 September 1921, Z. 4760/Fra, *NPA Karton* 326.

43. *BMfHW* to Liq. Org., 28 September 1921, Z. 4896/Fra, *NPA Karton* 326.

44. Liq. Org. to chancellor and minister of foreign affairs, 24 October 1921, Z. 5732/Fra, *NPA Karton* 326. It is noteworthy that Hallier bypassed the ministry for military affairs, sending letters directly to the chancellor.

45. *BMfHW* to *BMfA*, 9 November 1921, Z. 6289/Fra, *NPA Karton* 326.

46. *BMfA* to *BMfHW*, 1 December 1921, Z. 6858/Fra, *NPA Karton* 326.

47. *BMfHW* to Liq. Org., 23 December 1921, Z. 7514/Fra, *NPA Karton* 326.

48. Liq. Org. to *BMfA*, 12 January 1923, Z. 186/Fra, *NPA Karton* 326.

49. *Bericht über die Tätigkeit des Heeresüberwachungsausschusses*, 1 May 1921, Z. 1936/Fra, *NPA Karton* 367.

50. BAFR, 21 August 1920, F.O. 371/4643 (C-5416).

51. BAFR, 12 September 1920, F.O. 371/4643 (C-7338).

52. See chap. 2 above for a discussion of Frey's role in the *Volkswehr*, p. 46.

53. BAFR, 12 September and 30 September 1920, F.O. 371/4643 (C-7338 and C-7850).

54. BAFR, 13 December 1920, F.O. 371/5747 (C-192).

55. C.A., 20 October 1920.

56. Zuccari note, 4 November 1920, Z. 4566/Fra, *NPA Karton* 322.

57. Eichoff to *BMfA*, 29 November 1920, Z. 5014/Fra, *NPA Karton* 322.

58. C.A., 27 December 1920.

59. Lindley to Curzon, 15 November 1920, printed in *DBFP*, 12:334–35.

60. Lindley to Curzon, 6 November 1920, F.O. 371/4644 (C-11343).

61. BAFR, 13 December 1920, F.O. 371/5747 (C-192).

62. BAFR, 26 May 1921, F.O. 371/5747 (C-12270).

63. BAFR, 16 November 1921, F.O. 371/5748 (C-22057).

64. BAFR, 15 September 1921, F.O. 371/5748 (C-18368).

65. BAFR, 16 November 1921, F.O. 371/5748 (C-22057).

66. C.A., 2 December 1920.

67. Ibid.

68. Zuccari to *BmfA* and *BMfHW,* 20 December 1920, Z. 5226/Fra, *NPA Karton* 326.

69. *StAfHW* to Hallier, 31 January 1921, Z. 445/Fra, *NPA Karton* 326; *StAfA* to Eichoff, 14 February 1921, Z. 498/Fra, *NPA Karton* 326.

70. Memo for *Ministerrat,* 9 March 1921, Z. 1000/Fra, and *BMfHW* to *BMfA,* 15 March 1921, Z. 1102/Fra, *NPA Karton* 326.

71. *StAfHW* to *StAfA,* 19 March 1921, Z. 1147/Fra, *NPA Karton* 326.

72. Hallier to *BMfA,* 25 March 1921, Z. 1248/Fra, and *StAfHW* to *StAfA,* 6 April 1921, Z. 1409/Fra, *NPA Karton* 326.

73. Briand to Eichoff, 6 April 1921, Z. 1610/Fra, *NPA Karton* 326.

74. *StAfA* to *StAfHW,* 14 April 1921, Z. 1495/Fra, *NPA Karton* 326.

75. *BMfHW* to *BMfA,* 12 April 1921, Z. 1495/Fra, *NPA Karton* 326.

76. Liq. Org. to Mayr, 27 April 1921, Z. 1718/Fra, *NPA Karton* 326.

77. BAFR, 15 June 1921, F.O. 371/5747 (C-13157).

78. Liq. Org. to *StAfA,* 6 July 1921, Z. 3084/Fra, and Liq. Org. to *BMfA,* 26 July 1921, Z. 3489/Fra, *NPA Karton* 326.

79. BAFR, 5 August 1921, F.O. 371/5748 (C-16447).

80. BAFR, 7 April 1920, F.O. 371/3537 (191478). Socialist sympathy for the retention of excess police was based in part on the fact that the overcomplement had been recruited from the *Volkswehr* and therefore represented a socialist element in the generally conservative police forces. Details concerning the recruiting of these men were discussed above in chap. 2, p. 49.

81. BAFR, 12 September 1920, F.O. 371/4643 (C-7338).

82. BAFR, 13 December 1920, F.O. 371/5747 (C-192).

83. C.A., 22 December 1920; Hallier to *BMfI,* 5 January 1921, Z. 648/Fra, *NPA Karton* 326.

84. *BMfI* to Hallier, 11 January and 17 January 1921, Z. 20901/Fra, *NPA Karton* 326.

85. C.A., 9 February 1921; *BMfHW* to *BMfA,* 14 February 1921, Z. 633/Fra, *NPA Karton* 329.

86. Frazier to State, 7 May 1921, M-695, roll 21 (863.20/7).

87. Ibid.

88. Frazier to State, 19 May 1921, M-695, roll 21 (863.20/8).

89. BAFR, 26 May 1921, F.O. 371/5747 (C-12270).

90. C.A., 3 June 1921.

91. Liq. Org. to *BMfA,* 28 December 1921, Z. 7659/Fra, *NPA Karton* 329.

92. BAFR, 12 September 1920, F.O. 371/4643 (C-7338).

93. BAFR, 17 February 1921, F.O. 371/5747 (C-4737).

94. Ibid.

95. BAFR, 9 July 1921, F.O. 371/5747 (C-15583).

96. BAFR, 16 November 1921, F.O. 371/5748 (C-22057).

97. Liq. Org. to *BMfA,* 17 March 1922, Z. 1017/Fra, *NPA Karton* 329.

98. BAFR, 10 December 1921, F.O. 371/5748 (C-23643).

99. Raymond E. Bell, Jr., "A Unionized Army in Battle: The Burgenland Action," *History, Numbers, and War* 1 (1977): 186–89.

Chapter 7. The Spoils of War

1. *Bericht über die Tätigkeit des Heeresüberwachungsausschusses,* 1 May 1921, Z. 1936/Fra, *NPA Karton* 367.
2. C.A., 9 December 1920.
3. H.D., 25 July 1919.
4. H.D., 1 August 1919.
5. See C.F., 9 June 1919, and H.D., 25 July 1919. The reference on 9 June to the arms transfer was oblique, inserted briefly in the midst of a discussion of the Rumanian-Hungarian-Czechoslovak hostilities. The remark would have been easy to overlook.
6. BAFR, 3 February 1920, F.O. 371/3534 (178580).
7. BAFR, 16 February 1920, F.O. 371/3535 (181524).
8. BAFR, 3 February 1920, F.O. 371/3534 (178580).
9. BAFR, 27 April 1920, F.O. 371/3538 (198036).
10. BAFR, 7 June 1920, F.O. 371/3538 (20453).
11. Longare to Millerand, 9 March 1920 (Appendix E to C.A., 1 April 1920).
12. C.A., 1 April 1920.
13. C.A., 4 May 1920.
14. C.A., 19 May 1920.
15. BAFR, 22 May 1920, F.O. 371/3538 (201947); C.A., 26 May 1920.
16. C.A., 5 June 1920 (P.M.).
17. C.A., 23 June 1920.
18. Excerpt from C.A., 8 October 1920, M-820, roll 381 (185.2151/45).
19. C.A., 27 October 1920.
20. C.A., 24 November 1920.
21. C.A., 8 October 1920.
22. C.A., 24 November 1920.
23. C.A., 9 December 1920.
24. Ibid.
25. C.A., 15 December 1920.
26. Ibid.
27. Ibid.
28. C.A., 27 December 1920.
29. C.A., 22 December 1920.
30. C.A., 2 February 1921.
31. *Fliegen 90/71* (Vienna, 1971), pp. 220–21.
32. C.A., 10 February 1920.
33. C.A., 2 December 1920.
34. C.A., 1 May 1920; 24 November 1920.
35. C.A., 29 September 1920.
36. C.A., 24 November 1920.
37. C.A., 20 October 1920.
38. BAFR, 25 October 1920, F.O. 371/4643 (C-10374).
39. Deutsch to Renner, c. 23 March 1920, z. 1167/Fra, *NPA Karton* 366.
40. The exact cost of the Control Commissions has not been calculated, and probably cannot be. The soaring inflation of Austrian currency makes Deutsch's assertion plausible.
41. BAFR, 21 November 1920, F.O. 371/4644 (C-12436).
42. C.A., 2 December 1920.

43. C.A., 12 January 1921.

44. Austrian liaison office (signature illegible) to *BMfA*, 21 December 1920, Z. 5219/ Fra, *NPA Karton* 366.

45. C.A., 22 January 1921.

46. C.A., 2 February 1921; C.A., 9 February 1921.

47. Foch to ICC, 14 February 1921, *NPA Karton* 367 (folio 188).

48. C.A., 17 February 1921.

49. C.A., 2 March 1921.

50. BAFR, 17 March 1921, F.O. 371/5747 (C-6172).

51. Liq. Org. to *BMfA*, 10 March 1921, Z. 1093/Fra, *NPA Karton* 367.

52. Gosset to *BMfA*, 13 May 1921, Z. 1975/Fra, *NPA Karton* 367.

53. BAFR, 2 March 1921, F.O. 371/5747 (C-6171); Memo for chancellor, 19 February 1921, Z. 694/Fra, *NPA Karton* 366; police commissioner of Wiener Neustadt to *BMfI*, 19 February 1921, Z. 878/Fra, *NPA Karton* 367.

54. BAFR, 2 March 1921, F.O. 371/5747 (C-6171).

55. For example, Hallier to *BMfA*, 28 February 1921, Z. 873/Fra, *NPA Karton* 326.

56. For example, C.A., 1 April 1921.

Chapter 8. A House Divided

1. Haas, "Wehrpolitik," pp. 28–29.

2. Reinhart Kondert, "The Rise and Early History of the Austrian Heimwehr," (Ph.D. diss. Rice University, 1972), p. 2; Edmondson, *Heimwehr*, p. 270 n. 6.

3. Kondert, "Heimwehr," pp. 18–21.

4. F. L. Carsten, *Fascist Movements in Austria: From Schönerer to Hitler* (London, 1977), p. 44.

5. Ibid.

6. Edmondson, *Heimwehr*, p. 22.

7. Swedish legation to State, 7 December 1918, and Polk to House, 10 December 1918, printed in *FRUS-PPC*, 2:199 and 201.

8. Swedish legation to State, 13 December 1918, printed in *FRUS-PPC*, 2:202–3.

9. Steinböck, *Kämpfe im Raum Völkermarkt*, pp. 5–30.

10. Edmondson, *Heimwehr*, p. 20. The seeds of partisan conflict were certainly present even though the Austrian political differences were smoothed over during the fighting. Kondert mentions that the fight against the Slavs brought volunteers from Bavaria, foreshadowing a more ominous association. (Kondert, "Heimwehr," p. 9.

11. DuBois to State, 12 September 1919, printed in *FRUS-PPC*, 12:568.

12. BAFR, 15 December 1919, F.O. 371/3533 (166612).

13. BAFR: 3 February 1920, F.O. 371/3534 (178580); 15 March 1920, F.O. 371/3536 (189157); 18 March 1920, F.O. 371/3536 (189156).

14. BAFR: 27 March 1920, F.O. 371/3536 (190001); 10 April 1920, F.O. 371/3537 (193648).

15. Kondert, "Heimwehr," pp. 6–16.

16. Ibid., pp. 21–22.

17. Goggia (chief of Italian Mission) to *StAfHW*, 9 April 1920, *NPA Karton* 366 (Konv. I, folio 85). This letter refers to earlier messages in December 1919.

18. C.A., 14 February 1920.

19. Lindley to Curzon, 19 January 1920, printed in *DBFP*, 12:88.

20. C.A., 14 February 1920.

21. Gosset to War Office, 24 April 1920, F.O. 371/3537 (194440).

22. BAFR, 6 April 1920, F.O. 371/3536 (190800).

23. Gosset to War Office, 11 June 1920; Cuninghame to Lindley, 17 June 1920; Lindley to Curzon, 18 June 1920; all in F.O. 371/3538 (205421).

24. BAFR, 9 November 1920, F.O. 371/4644 (C-11812).

25. BAFR, 13 December 1920, F.O. 371/5747 (C-192).

26. C.A., 15 December 1920; Briand to Eichoff, 23 December 1920, *NPA Karton* 326 (Konv. II, folio 367).

27. BAFR, 4 January 1921, F.O. 371/5747 (C-1169).

28. Liq. Org. to Mayr, 1 March 1921, Z. 947/Fra, *NPA Karton* 330.

29. *BMfI* and *BMfU* to *BMfA,* 15 March 1921, Z. 1101/Fra, *NPA Karton* 330.

30. Liq. Org. to Mayr, 22 March 1921, Z. 1186/Fra, *NPA Karton* 330.

31. BAFR, 17 March 1921, F.O. 371/5747 (C-6172).

32. BAFR, 6 April 1921, F.O. 371/5747 (C-7862).

33. Liq. Org. to Chancellor, 4 July 1921, Z. 3083/Fra, *NPA Karton* 330.

34. Liq. Org. to Chancellor, 9 June 1921, Z. 2505/Fra, *NPA Karton* 330; BAFR, 15 June 1921, F.O. 371/5747 (C-13157); Liq. Org. to Chancellor, 29 June 1921, Z. 2925/Fra, *NPA Karton* 330; C.A., 17 August 1921; C.A. to Eichoff, 27 August 1921, enclosure in dispatch to State, 8 November 1921, M-695, roll 21 (863.20/9); Liq. Org. to Chancellor, 1 September 1921, Z. 4275/Fra, *NPA Karton* 330.

35. Liq. Org. to Chancellor, 19 December 1921, Z. 7402/Fra, *NPA Karton* 330.

36. For example: Liq. Org. to *BMfA*, 12 April 1922, Nr. 670/DOL, NPA Karton 330; Liq. Org. to Chancellor, 8 May 1922, Nr. 705/DOL, *NPA Karton* 330.

37. C.A., 12 November 1920.

38. C.A., 2 February 1921.

39. BAFR, 16 November 1921, F.O. 371/5748 (C-22057).

40. BAFR, 4 January 1921, F.O. 371/5747 (C-1169).

41. BAFR, 26 May 1921, F.O. 371/5747 (C-12270).

Bibliography

1

Unpublished Primary Materials

Allgemeines Verwaltungsarchiv

Kabinettsprotokolle (October 1918–November 1920).
Ministerratsprotokolle (November 1920–December 1922).
Staatsratprotokolle (1918–19).

Haus-, Hof-, und Staatsarchiv
(Neues Politisches Archiv)

Karton 322: Miscellaneous military issues, including *Volkswehr* reports and the militia question.

Karton 326: Military questions 1919–21, dealing mostly with correspondence concerning Allied Control Commissions.

Karton 328: Documents relating to *Volkswehr* reduction and relations with the Italian Armistice Commission.

Karton 329: Issues concerning the police and the gendarmerie.

Karton 330: Problems regarding disarming civilians, 1921–34.

Karton 331: Biweekly reports on the progress of disarming the population, May 1921 through December 1922.

Karton 333: Documents relative to Austrian Federal Army action in the Burgenland.

Karton 334: Documents relative to the manufacture of war equipment.

Karton 365: Documents relative to early missions in Austria, including the Coolidge mission.

Karton 366–67: Correspondence regarding Allied Control Commissions.

150

Karton 370: Documents relative to the armistice and relations with Italy.

Karton 374 and 376: The Austrian delegation at the Peace Conference.

Karton 379 through 387: War matériel and aeronautical problems.

Karton 388: Issue of cost of the Inter-Allied Control Commissions.

Hoover Institution on War, Revolution, and Peace
(Stanford, California)

Conference of Ambassadors, Minutes of the Paris Meetings. Mimeographed typewritten manuscript. (Also available in the U.S. National Archives, Record Group 256, Microcopy 820, rolls 57–106.)

Conference Bulletins.

Daily Bulletins. Issued by Military Information Section, nos. 27–114 (17 February–29 May 1919).

S-H Bulletins (1919). Supreme War Council and negotiations concerning Saint Germain, nos. 5, 6, 7, 59, 63, 306, 356, 381, 516, 537, and 668.

ESH Bulletins (1920). Military clauses of Saint Germain and disposition of Austrian war matériel, nos. 93, 625, 720, 781, 925, and 1344.

Fuller Papers, B.A.G. Fuller Collection. Box 5 includes some documents relative to the Austrian military situation in 1918–19.

Stockton Papers, Gilcrest Baker Stockton Collection. Box 8 includes Stockton's correspondence from Vienna, where he was head of relief operations under the American Relief Administration.

Kriegsarchiv
(Archiv des Österreichischen Bundesheers 1918–19)

"Provisorische deutschösterreichische Wehrmacht, 1918–1920."

Fasz.: "Oberbefehlshaber der deutschösterreichischen Wehrmacht."

"Registratur des Staatsamtes für Heerwesen."

Fasz. 1: "Waffenstillstandkom., 1919." Documents relative to Italian Armistice Commission.

Fasz. 2: "Waffenstillstand, 1920–1921." Documents relative to Inter-Allied Control Commissions.

Fasz. 3: "B.M.f.L.V., Sekt. II, Waffenstillstand u. Interallierte 1919–1921." Documents relative to the army question.

Fasz., unnumbered: "B.M.f.L.V., Sekt. II, 1921–1923." Documents relative to Inter-Allied Control Commissions.

"Zur Geschichte des Österreichischen Bundesheers."

Fasz. 1: Documents relative to the Treaty of Saint Germain and the Liquidation Commission.

Fasz. 1a: Documents relative to negotiations concerning the Treaty of Saint Germain.

Fasz. 2: Austrian studies relating to the future Federal Army and some documents on *Volkswehr* matters.

Fasz. 6: Documents relative to Inter-Allied Control Commissions.

Public Record Office
(British Foreign Office Records)

F.O. 371/3533 through 3538: covers Austrian affairs, January–June 1920.

F.O. 371/4643 and 4644: covers Austrian affairs, July–November 1920.

F.O. 371/5747 and 5748: covers Austrian affairs, January–December 1921.

U.S. National Archives

Department of State, Record Group 256.

Microcopy 695, roll 21: records relating to military affairs in Austria, 1910–29.

Microcopy 820, roll 127: minutes of the Supreme War Council.

Microcopy 820, rolls 178–79: negotiations, Treaty of Saint Germain.

Microcopy 820, rolls 203–13: administration of and reports from the Coolidge Mission to Austria.

Microcopy 820, rolls 214–16: reports from the Halstead Mission to Austria.

Microcopy 820, rolls 381–82: excerpts of documents relating to military clauses of Saint Germain and relating to the Inter-Allied Control Commissions.

Navy and Old Army Branch, Military Intelligence Division Files.

M.I.D. 2540: Documents relative to Austrian army after 1918.

M.I.D. 2657: Documents relative to the political dimensions of Austrian military affairs, especially paramilitary groups.

M.I.D. 2724: Documents relative to disarmament problems in Austria.

M.I.D. 2736: Documents relative to military trade unions and labor unions in Austria.

2
Published Documents

Official Documents

Austria. *Bericht über die Tätigkeit der deutschösterreichischen Friedensdelegation in St. Germain-en-Laye.* 2 vols. Vienna: Staatsdruckerei, 1919.

Austria. *Stenographische Protokolle über die Sitzungen der Konstituierenden Nationalversammlung der Republik Österreich, 1919–1920.* Vienna: Staatsdruckerei, 1919–20.

Austria. *Stenographische Protokolle über die Sitzungen der Provisorischen Nationalversammlung für Deutschösterreich, 1918–1919.* Vienna: Staatsdruckerei, 1919.

Great Britain. Foreign Office. *Documents on British Foreign Policy.* First Series. 21 vols. London: HMSO, 1947–78.

U.S. Department of State. *Papers Relating to the Foreign Relations of the United States, 1918.* Supplement 1. 2 vols. Washington, D.C.: GPO, 1933.

U.S. Department of State. *Papers Relating to the Foreign Relations of the United States, 1919: The Paris Peace Conference.* 13 vols. Washington, D.C.: GPO, 1942–47.

Documentary Collections

Almond, Nina, and Ralph Haswell Lutz, eds. *The Treaty of St. Germain: A Documentary History of Its Territorial and Political Clauses.* Hoover War Library Publication No. 5. Stanford, Calif.: Stanford University Press, 1935.

Miller, David Hunter. *My Diary at the Conference of Paris, With Documents.* 21 vols. New York: Appeal Printing Co., 1924.

Neck, Rudolf, ed. *Österreich im Jahre 1918: Berichte und Dokumente.* Vienna: Verlag für Geschichte und Politik Wien, 1968.

3
Secondary Literature

Albrecht-Carrié, René. *Italy at the Peace Conference.* New York: Columbia University Press, 1938. Reprint. Hamden, Conn.: Archon Books, 1966.

Allmayer-Beck, Johann Christoph. "Das österreichische Bundesheer."

In *1918–1968 Österreich: 50 Jahre Republik.* Vienna: Institut für Österreichkunde, 1968.

Andics, Hellmut. *Der Staat den Keiner Wollte: Österreich 1918–1938.* Vienna: Verlag Herder, 1962.

Artofer, Hans. *1918–1936, Vom Selbstschutz zur Frontmiliz.* Vienna: Zoller & Co., 1937.

Auffenberg-Komarów, Mortiz. *Oesterreich und das Problem seiner Landesverteidigung: Ein Vortrag in der oesterreichischen politischen Gesellschaft in Wien am 16. Dezember 1924.* Vienna: Josef Lenobel, 1925.

Barker, Elisabeth. *Austria: 1918–1972.* Coral Gables, Fla.: University of Miami Press, 1973.

Bauer, Otto. *The Austrian Revolution.* Translated by H. J. Stenning. London: L. Parsons, 1925.

———. *Die österreichische Revolution.* Vienna: Wiener Volksbuchhandlung, 1923.

———. *Die Offiziere und die Republik: Ein Vortrag über die Wehrpolitik der Sozialdemokratie.* Vienna: Wiener Volksbuchhandlung, 1921.

Bell, Raymond E., Jr. "A Unionized Army in Battle: The Burgenland Action." *History, Numbers and War* 1 (1977): 182–93.

Benedikt, Heinrich, ed. *Geschichte der Republik Österreich.* Munich: Verlag R. Oldenbourg, 1954.

Blenk, Gustav. *Leopold Kunschak und seine Zeit: Porträt eines christlichen Arbeiterführers.* Vienna: Europa Verlag, 1966.

Boese, Hartmut W. "Die Zusammenarbeit von Bundesheer, Heimwehr und Schutzbund in Tirol 1925/1926." University of Vienna, 1967. Photocopy.

Böhm, Erich. "Das österreichische Bundesheer 1920–1938." *Feldgrau* 7 (1959): 33–36, 87–93, 121–23, 154–58, 181–82, 186–91.

Bosek, Eva. "Die diplomatischen Beziehungen zwischen Österreich und Grossbritannien (1922–1924)." Ph.D. diss., University of Vienna, 1975.

Bosl, Karl, ed. *Versailles-St. Germain-Trianon: Umbruch im Europa vor fünfzig Jahren.* Munich and Vienna: R. Oldenbourg, 1971.

Botz, Gerhard. *Gewalt in der Politik: Attentate, Zusammenstösse, Putschversuche, Unruhen in Österreich 1918 bis 1934.* Munich: Wilhelm Fink Verlag, 1976.

Braunthal, Julius. *In Search of the Millennium.* London: Victor Gollancz, Ltd., 1945.

———. *The Tragedy of Austria.* London: Victor Gollancz, Ltd., 1948.

Carsten, F. L. *Fascist Movements in Austria: From Schönerer to Hitler.* London: SAGE Publications Ltd., 1977.

―――. *Revolution in Central Europe: 1918–1919.* Berkeley and Los Angeles: University of California Press, 1972.

Deutsch, Julius. *Aus Österreichs Revolution: Militärpolitische Erinnerungen.* Vienna: Verlag der Wiener Volksbuchhandlung, [1921].

―――. *Wehrmacht und Sozialdemokratie.* Berlin: J. H. W. Dietz Nachf., 1928.

―――. *Ein Weiter Weg: Lebenserinnerungen.* Zurich: Amalthea-Verlag, 1960.

Duczynska, Ilona. *Der demokratische Bolschewik: Zur Theorie und Praxis der Gewalt.* Munich: Paul List Verlag, 1975.

―――. *Theodor Körner: Auf Vorposten Ausgewählte Schriften 1928–1938.* Vienna: Europaverlag, 1977.

Edmondson, C. Earl. "Early Heimwehr Aims and Activities." *Austrian History Yearbook* 7 (1972): 105–47.

―――. *The Heimwehr and Austrian Politics, 1918–1936.* Athens: University of Georgia Press, 1978.

Eisenmenger, Anna. *Blockade: The Diary of an Austrian Middle-Class Woman, 1914–1924.* New York: Ray Long & Richard R. Smith, Inc., 1932.

Fellner, Fritz, ed. *Schicksalsjahre Österreichs, 1908–1919: Das politische Tagebuch Josef Redlichs.* 2 vols. Graz and Cologne: Verlag Hermann Böhlaus Nachf., 1953–54.

Freise, Ursula. "Die Tätigkeit der allierten Kommissionen in Wien nach dem ersten Weltkrieg." Ph.D. diss., University of Vienna, 1963.

Fritz, Friedrich. *Der deutsche Einmarsch in Österreich 1938.* Militärhistorische Schriftenreihe, 8. By Heeresgeschichtliches Museum/Militärwissenschaftliches Institut. Vienna: Österreichischer Bundesverlag für Unterricht, Wissenschaft und Kunst, 1968.

Führ, Christoph. *Das k.u.k. Armeeoberkommando und die Innenpolitik in Österreich 1914–1917.* Studien zur Geschichte der österreichisch-ungarischen Monarchie, 7. Graz: Hermann Böhlaus Nachf., 1968.

Funder, Friedrich. *From Empire to Republic.* Translated by Barbara Waldstein. New York: A. Unger Publishing Co., 1963.

―――. *Vom Gestern ins Heute: Aus dem Kaiserreich in die Republik.* Vienna and Munich: Verlag Herald, 1952.

Glaise-Horstenau, Edmund von. *The Collapse of the Austro-Hungarian Empire.* Translated by Ian F. D. Morrow. London and Toronto: J. M. Dent and Sons, 1930.

Gruber, Ferdinand. "Der Kärntner Freiheitskampf 1918/1919." *Militärwissenschaftliche und technische Mitteilungen*(1922): 429–46.

Gschaider, Peter. "Das österreichische Bundesheer 1938 und seine Überführung in die deutsche Wehrmacht." Ph.D. diss., University of Vienna, 1967.

Gulick, Charles Adams. *Austria from Habsburg to Hitler.* 2 vols. Berkeley and Los Angeles: University of California Press, 1948.

Haas, Hanns. "Österreich-Ungarn als Friedensproblem: Aspekte der Friedensregelung auf dem Gebiet der Habsburgermonarchie in den Jahren 1918–1919." Ph.D. diss., University of Salzburg, 1968.

Haas, Karl. "Studien zur Wehrpolitik der österreichischen Sozialdemokratie 1918–1926." Ph.D. diss., University of Vienna, 1967.

———. "Zur Wehrpolitik der österreichischen Sozialdemokratie in der ersten Republik." *Truppendienst* 2 (1973): 105–8.

Handbuch der Bewaffneten Macht. Vienna: Bundesministerium für Landesverteidigung, 1937.

Hanks, Ronald. "The End of an Institution: The Austro-Hungarian Army in Italy, 1918." Ph.D. diss., Rice University, 1977.

Hantsch, Hugo. "Der Friede von St. Germain 1919," *Österreichische Militärische Zeitschrift* 5 (1969): 353–56.

Hasenhündl, Gerhard. "Körperliche Ertüchtigung und Sport im Bundesheer der ersten Republik." University of Vienna, 1977. Photocopy.

———. "Das Rätewesen im österreichischen Bundesheer der 1. Republik." University of Vienna, 1977. Photocopy.

Hausmann, Astrid. "Die amerikanische Aussenpolitik und die Entstehung der Republik Österreich von 1917–1919." Ph.D. diss., University of Vienna, 1973.

Hecht, Rudolf. "Die Wehrpolitik der österreichischen Regierung von 1919 bis 1934." University of Vienna, 1965. Photocopy.

Hoffmann, Robert. "The British Military Representative in Vienna, 1919." *Slavonic and East European Review* 52 (1974): 252–71.

———. "Die Mission Sir Thomas Cuninghames in Wien 1919: Britische Österreichpolitik zur Zeit der Pariser Friedenskonferenz." Ph.D. diss., University of Salzburg, 1971.

Huemer, Peter. *Sektionschef Robert Hecht und die Zerstörung der Demokratie in Österreich: Eine historisch-politische Studie.* Vienna: Verlag für Geschichte und Politik Wien, 1975.

Jedlicka, Ludwig. *Vom alten zum neuen Österreich: Fallstudien zur österreichischen Zeitgeschichte 1900–1975.* St. Pölten and Vienna: Verlag Niederösterreichisches Pressehaus, 1975.

————. *Ein Heer im Schatten der Parteien: Die militärpolitische Lage Österreichs 1918–1938.* Graz and Cologne: Hermann Böhlaus Nachf., 1955.

————. "Die Tradition der Wehrmacht Österreichs-Ungarns und die Nachfolgestaaten." *Österreichische Militärische Zeitschrift* 6 (1968): 441–47.

———— and Anton Staudinger. *Ende und Anfang: Österreich 1918/1919.* Salzburg: SN Verlag, 1969.

Jlaskal, Ludwig von. *Die Entwicklung des Militär-Kraftfahrwesens in Österreich vom März 1898 bis März 1938.* Vienna: Österreichischen Automobil-Motorrad-u. Touring-Club, 1960.

Kann, Robert A., Béla K. Király, and Paula S. Fichtner, eds. *The Habsburg Empire in World War I: Essays on the Intellectual, Military, Political and Economic Aspects of the Habsburg War Effort.* Brooklyn College Studies on Society in Change. Vol 2. New York: Columbia University Press, 1977.

Keynes, John Maynard. *The Economic Consequences of the Peace.* London: Macmillan and Co., 1919.

Kleinfeld, Gerald. "Stabilization and Reconstruction in Austria: Schober and Seipel 1921–1922." Ph.D. diss., New York University, 1961.

Kleinwaechter, Friedrich F. G. *Von Schönbrunn bis St. Germain: Die Entstehung der Republik Österreich.* Graz, Vienna, and Cologne: Verlag Styria, 1964.

Klemperer, Klemens von. "Austria, 1918–1920: Revolution by Consensus." *Orbis* 10 (1967): 1061–81.

————. *Ignaz Seipel: Christian Statesman in a Time of Crisis.* Princeton, N.J.: Princeton University Press, 1972.

Körner, Theodor. *Denkschrift über das Heerwesen der Republik.* Vienna: Verlag des Militärbandes, 1924.

Kollman, Eric C. *Theodor Körner: Militär und Politik.* Vienna: Verlag für Geschichte und Politik Wien, 1973.

Kondert, Reinhard. "The Rise and Early History of the Austrian Heimwehr Movement." Ph.D. diss., Rice University, 1972.

Kreissler, Felix. *Von der Revolution zur Annexion: Österreich 1918 bis 1938.* Vienna, Frankfurt, and Zurich: Europa Verlag, 1970.

Kreuter, Siegburt. "Führende österreichische Sozialdemokraten und die Wehrfrage." *Österreichische Militärische Zeitschrift* 3 (1974): 181–90.

Kromer, Claudia. *Die Vereinigten Staaten von Amerika und die Frage Kärnten 1918–1920.* Klagenfurt: Geschichtsverein für Kärnten, 1970.

Lafleur, Ingrun. "Socialists, Communists and Workers in the Austrian Revolution, 1918–1919." Ph.D. diss., Columbia University, 1972.

Large, David C. "The Politics of Law and Order: Counterrevolutionary 'Self-Defence' Organizations in Central Europe, 1918–1923." Ph.D. diss., University of California (Berkeley), 1974.

Lederer, Ivo J. *Yugoslavia at the Paris Peace Conference: A Study in Frontiermaking.* New Haven, Conn.: Yale University Press, 1963.

Low, Alfred D. *The Anschluss Movement, 1918–1919 and the Paris Peace Conference.* Philadelphia: American Philosophical Society, 1974.

————. "The First Austrian Republic and Soviet Hungary." *Journal of Central European Affairs* 20, (1960): 174–203.

Macartney, C. A. *The Social Revolution in Austria.* Cambridge: At the University Press, 1926.

MacDonald, Mary. *The Republic of Austria, 1918–1934: A Study in the Failure of Democratic Government.* London: Oxford University Press, 1946.

Mamatey, Victor S. *The United States and East-Central Europe, 1914–1918: A Study in Wilsonian Diplomacy and Propaganda.* Princeton, N.J.: Princeton University Press, 1957.

Mantoux, Etienne. *The Carthaginian Peace, or the Economic Consequences of Mr. Keynes.* London: Oxford University Press, 1946.

Maurice, Sir Frederick. *The Armistices of 1918.* London: Oxford University Press, 1943.

May, Arthur J. *The Passing of the Hapsburg Monarchy, 1914–1918.* 2 vols. Philadelphia: University of Pennsylvania Press, 1966.

Mayer, Arno J. *Politics and Diplomacy of Peacemaking: Containment and Counterrevolution at Versailles, 1918–1919.* New York: Alfred A. Knopf, 1967.

Militärluftfahrt und Luftabwehr in Österreich von 1890 bis 1971. Vol. 1 of *Fliegen 90/71.* Vienna: Heeresgeschichtliches Museum/ Militärwissenschaftliches Institut, 1971.

Mitrany, David. *The Effect of the War in Southeastern Europe.* New Haven, Conn.: Yale University Press, 1936.

Nicolson, Harold. *Peacemaking 1919.* London: Constable and Co., 1933.

1918–1968: Die Streitkräfte der Republik Österreich. Vienna: Heeresgeschichtliches Museum/Militärwissenschaftliches Institut, 1968.

"Das österreichische Bundesheer." Special edition of *Österreichische Illustrierte Zeitung,* No. 37, 1 July 1927.

Österreichs Bundesheer. By Bundesministerium für Heereswesen. Vienna: Militärwissenschaftliche und technische Mitteilungen, [1929].

Osterreich-Ungarns Letzter Krieg, 1914–1918. 7 vols. By Bundesministerium für Heereswesen (Bundesministerium für Landesverteidigung after 1933), and Kriegsarchiv. Vienna: Verlag der Militärwissenschaftlichen Mitteilungen, 1931–1938.

Pauley, Bruce F. *The Habsburg Legacy 1867–1939.* The Berkshire Studies in European History. New York: Holt, Rinehart & Winston, 1972. Reprint. Huntington, N.Y.: Robert E. Krieger Publishing Co., 1977.

———. *Hahnenschwanz und Hakenkreuz: Steierischer Heimatschutz und österreichischer Nationalsozialismus 1918–1934.* Vienna, Munich, and Zurich: Europaverlag, 1972.

Plaschka, Richard G. *Cattaro–Prag: Revolte und Revolution.* Graz and Cologne: Hermann Böhlaus Nachf., 1963.

——— and Karlheinz Mack, eds. *Die Auflösung des Habsburgerreiches: Zusammenbruch und Neuorientlerung im Donauraum.* Schriftenreihe des österreichischen Ost- und Südosteuropa- Instituts, 3. Munich: R. Oldenbourg Verlag, 1970.

Rauchensteiner, Manfried, and Erwin Pitsch. *Die Stiftskaserne in Krieg und Frieden.* Die Kasernen Österreichs, 1. By Heeresgeschichtliches Museum/Militärwissenschaftliches Institut. Vienna: Bundesministerium für Landesverteidigung, 1977.

Redlich, Joseph. *Austrian War Government.* New Haven, Conn.: Yale University Press, 1929.

Regele, Oskar. *Feldmarschall Conrad: Auftrag und Erfüllung 1906–1918.* Vienna: Herold, 1955.

Reichhold, Ludwig. *Scheidewege einer Republik: Österreich 1918–1968.* Vienna: Verlag Herder, 1968.

Roegelsperger, Helga. "Die Politik Frankreichs gegenüber Österreich von 1918–1922." Ph.D. diss., University of Vienna, 1973.

Rothenberg, Gunter E. "The Army of Austria-Hungary, 1868–1918: A Case Study of a Multi-ethnic Force." In *New Dimensions in Military History: An Anthology.* Edited by Russell F. Weigley. San Rafael, Calif.: Presidio Press, 1975.

———. *The Army of Francis Joseph.* Lafayette, Ind.: Purdue University Press, 1976.

Schäfer, Theo. "Die Genesis der Anschlussbewegung und die Anschlussdiplomatie 1918–1919." Ph.D. diss., University of Vienna, 1970.

Schlag, Gerald. *Die Kämpfe um das Burgenland 1921.* Militärhistorische Schriftenreihe, 16. By Heeresgeschichtliches Museum/ Militärwissenschaftliches Institut. Vienna: Österreichischer Bundesverlag für Unterricht, Wissenschaft und Kunst, 1970.

Schlemlein, Adolf von. *Carl Vaugoin: 10 Jahre Bundesheer, 1921–1931.* Vienna: Privately printed, 1932.

Sozius (Eli Rubin). *Carl Vaugoin: der Aufstieg einer Armee.* Vienna: Volkschriften Verlag, 1931.

Stadler, Karl R. *The Birth of The Austrian Republic, 1918–1921.* Leyden: A. W. Sijthoff, 1966.

Staudinger, Anton. "Bemühungen Carl Vaugoins um Suprematie der christlichsozialen Partei in Österreich (1930–1933)." Ph.D. diss., University of Vienna, 1969.

————. "Die Entstehung des Wehrgesetzes vom 18. März 1920." *Österreichische Militärische Zeitschrift* 2 (1970): 136–40.

————. "Die österreichische Wehrgesetzgebung 1918–1938" *Österreichische Militärische Zeitschrift* 3 (1971): 151–56; pt. 2: 4 (1971): 219–24.

Steinböck, Erwin. *Die Kämpfe im Raum Völkermarkt 1918/19.* Militärhistorische Schriftenreihe, 13. By Heeresgeschichtliches Museum/Militärwissenschaftliches Institut. Vienna: Österreichischer Bundesverlag für Unterricht, Wissenschaft und Kunst, 1969.

————. *Die Volkswehr in Kärnten unter Berücksichtigung des Einsatzes der Freiwilligenverbände.* Publikationen des österreichischen instituts für Zeitgeschichte, 2. Vienna and Graz: Stiasny Verlag, 1963.

Stone, Norman. "Army and Society in the Habsburg Monarchy, 1900–1914." *Past and Present* 33 (1966): 95–111.

————. *The Eastern Front 1914–1917.* New York: Charles Scribner's Sons, 1975.

Strong, David F. *Austria (October 1918–March 1919): Transition from Empire to Republic.* Studies in History, Economics and Public Law, no. 461. New York: Columbia University Press, 1939.

Taylor, A. J. P. *The Habsburg Monarchy, 1809–1918.* London: Hamish Hamilton, 1948. Reprint New York: Harper & Row, 1965.

Temperley, Harold W. V., ed. *A History of the Peace Conference of Paris.* 6 vols. London: Frowdy, Hodder, and Stoughton, 1920–24.

Tunstall, Graydon A. "The Schlieffen Plan: The Diplomacy and Military Strategy of the Central Powers in the East, 1905–1914." Ph.D. diss., Rutgers University, 1974.

Vaugoin, Karl. *Zur Denkschrift des Generals Körner: Die Antwort des Bundes-Ministers Vaugoin.* Vienna: Wehrbund, 1924.

Vidale, Emil. *Braucht Oesterreich die Wehrmacht? Ein Antrag auf Volksabstimmung.* Vienna: Rudolf Lechner & Sohn, 1925.

Wandycz, Piotr S. *France and Her Eastern Allies.* Minneapolis: University of Minnesota Press, 1962.

Weber, Friedrich. "Die Planungen des Deutsch-Österreichischen Staatsamtes für Heerwesen zur Aufstellung einer bewaffneten Macht vor Wirksamwerden der Bestimmungen des Friedensvertrages von St. Germain in den Jahren 1918 und 1919." From Heeresgeschichtliches Museum (Wissenschaftliches Institut). Militärwissenschaftliche Arbeit, 1978. Photocopy.

Wittas, Paul. *Unser Heer und seine Waffen.* Vienna: Hölder-Pichler-Tempsky, 1936.

Wutte, Martin. *Kärntens Freiheitskampf.* Klagenfurt: Ferd. Kleinmayr, 1922.

Zeman, Z. A. B. *The Break-Up of the Habsburg Empire, 1914–1918: A Study in National and Social Revolution.* London: Oxford University Press, 1961.

Zöllner, Erich. *Geschichte Österreichs: Von den Anfängen bis zur Gegenwart.* Munich: R. Oldenbourg Verlag, 1961.

Zorach, Jonathan. "The Czechoslovak Army, 1918–1938." Ph.D. diss., Columbia University, 1975.

Index